Bravo of the Brazos

The only known likeness of John Larn.

Bravo of the Brazos
John Larn of Fort Griffin, Texas

Robert K. DeArment

Foreword by Charles M. Robinson III

UNIVERSITY OF OKLAHOMA PRESS : NORMAN

Also by Robert K. DeArment
Bat Masterson: The Man and the Legend (Norman, 1979)
Knights of the Green Cloth: The Saga of the Frontier Gamblers (Norman, 1982)
George Scarborough: The Life and Death of a Lawman on the Closing Frontier (Norman, 1992)
(ed.) *Early Days in Texas: A Trip to Hell and Heaven, by Jim McIntire* (Norman, 1992)
Alias Frank Canton (Norman, 1996)
Deadly Dozen: Twelve Forgotten Gunfighters of the Old West (Norman, 2003)

Published with the assistance of the National Endowment for the Humanities, a federal agency which supports the study of such fields as history, philosophy, literature, and language.

Library of Congress Cataloging-in-Publication Data

DeArment, Robert K., 1925–
    Bravo of the Brazos : John Larn of Fort Griffin, Texas/ Robert K. DeArment ; foreword by Charles M. Robinson III.
        p. cm.
    Includes bibliographical references and index.
    ISBN 978-0-8061-3714-8 (paper)
    1. Larn, John M., d. 1878. 2. Outlaws—Texas—Fort Griffin—Biography. 3. Outlaws—Texas—Brazos River Valley—Biography. 4. Frontier and pioneer life—Texas—Fort Griffin. 5. Frontier and pioneer life—Texas—Brazos River Valley. 6. Fort Griffin (Tex.)—Biography. 7. Brazos River Valley (Tex.)—Biography. I. Title.

F394.F636 D43 2002
976.4'734—dc21   2002020555

Bravo:
A daring bandit, assassin or murderer

Brazos:
A river flowing SE from N. Texas to the Gulf of Mexico

The Random House Dictionary
of the English Language, Unabridged

Contents

Illustrations

Unless otherwise noted, all illustrations are from the author's personal collection.

Foreword

There are two kinds of Texas. One is the Texas of great cities—some with a sense of style that draws grudging approval even from Paris, and some that are infuriatingly shallow, faddish, and politically correct. The other Texas is found in the ranch country to the west, a region where the traditional ideals of family, honor, and community are zealously preserved.

Shackelford County, located some forty miles northeast of Abilene, is in the heart of this traditional Texas. Here, the sense of family, honor, and community centers around one name—John Larn, a man who died in 1878. It is strange that this should be so. Larn was a near contemporary of George Armstrong Custer, and the night he died, in a jail cell in Albany, is as remote from our own time as Custer's death at the Little Bighorn. Yet say his name in the coffee shop, and the room will divide between those who would overlook his many sins and those who say he got better than he deserved when a band of masked men pumped him full of lead.

Why does a man who has been dead so long, and was less than thirty years old when he died, arouse such emotion? It is because John Larn embodied the purest form of evil—he was a master of deception who left in his wake shattered families and ruined lives. Such pain carries across generations, and becomes especially acute when one considers the surprising longevity of Shackelford County residents. The children of the people Larn hurt lived well into the 1990s and suffered their parents' century-old grief until the end of their days.

Larn's career centered around what is called the Clear Fork Country, which is to say the region of the Clear Fork of the Brazos River in West Texas. In the 1870s the main settlement of the area was Fort Griffin, a town that grew up adjacent to the military post of the same name. The Flat, as the town was often called, ranked with Tombstone, Dodge City, and Deadwood as one of the meanest towns in the West. Its denizens read like a Who's Who of Western shootists and shady ladies. Pat Garrett was there, and so was John Selman. Likewise, Lottie Deno and "Big Nose" Kate Elder. Wyatt Earp claimed that he first met Doc Holliday at Fort Griffin, and the courthouse in Albany still preserves a docket that charged Doc with gambling in The Flat.

Locally, however, Larn looms larger than the rest. He was not an outlaw in the classic sense; outlaws often are outside the law for reasons over which they have no control, as was particularly true of Southerners during the years immediately following the Civil War. Larn was a badman, one who makes a conscious choice not only to operate outside the law, but to flaunt it at every turn. Even over a century later he is, in the words of one area citizen, "a pretty touchy subject."

Thus, as the twenty-first century began, the complete story remained to be told, and anyone who attempted it would find a daunting task. Part of the difficulty is due to Larn's own life, which was a maze of contradictions that created more questions than answers. A great deal more was due to the barriers erected in the Clear Fork Country, where the mention of his name drew anything from indulgent shrugs to open hostility—and usually from important people in Shackelford County. Some authors have skirted the issue, whereas others delved into it as best they could considering the circumstances under which each worked. Carl Coke Rister, whose *Fort Griffin on the Texas Frontier* was dedicated to Larn's nephew-in-law, Watt Matthews, gave the matter only passing reference. A Matthews relative later published what amounts to an apology for the entire Larn affair. Early in the twentieth century, however, Don H. Biggers discussed Larn's impact on the region in *Shackelford County Sketches*. In the decades that followed, Ben O. Grant, C. L. Sonnichsen, Frances Mayhugh Holden, Leon Metz, Ty Cashion, and, yes—even Charles Robinson—each built on Bigger's foundation, adding to the knowledge of the Larn affair. But a definitive biography remained to be written.[1]

Of particular interest was the question of who was involved in the Shackelford County Vigilance Committee and—by extension—in Larn's death. Most, including myself, sidestepped the matter. Although we had a good list of potential candidates, we did not have anything concrete. The times were such, and enough people were still alive that, as Sonnichsen once commented, a good list of potential candidates was not something to "leave lying around." Nor was it a good idea to dig too deeply, considering the people who could be hurt. The times just weren't right.

Fortunately, as the Larn affair receded further into the past and the times became right, Robert K. DeArment had already begun accumulating little known facts on Larn's life and career. There was no better man to tell the tale. Bob DeArment had already given Fort Griffin its due in *Knights of the Green Cloth*, his landmark study of Western gambling. And when it comes to gunfighters and badmen, I firmly believe that he and Leon Metz have the first, middle, and final word on the subject. The three of us discussed the need for a complete Larn biography during the 1998 meeting of the Western Writers of America in Colorado Springs. As I recall, much of the conversation centered around who should do it. I wasn't particularly interested, seeing how gunfighters and badmen are not my specialty. I already had given Larn's grave a pretty good shake with my book *The Frontier World of Fort Griffin*, as had Leon with *John Selman, Gunfighter* and *The Shootists*. It seemed to me that, deep down, Bob already intended to do it. At least, I went away hoping he did.

Now, we have the results of his efforts—an unvarnished biography of one of the West's least known and most vicious killers. Robert DeArment has traced John Larn as far as records will allow. He does not speculate on what might have triggered Larn's career of evil, but that is one of the great mysteries that may never be solved. On the other hand, DeArment has dug deeply into Larn's past, and the wall of silence in Shackelford County is beginning to crack. He has come as close as anyone likely will to answering other important questions, such as who was on the vigilance committee and who was involved in Larn's death. And while he has corrected many errors and misconceptions, he has also shown that the facts are even more amazing than the whispered stories.

CHARLES M. ROBINSON III

San Benito, Texas

Acknowledgments

No one writes the story of a man who has been dead for more than a century without relying heavily on the work of those who went before—the journalists, historical researchers, and authors who walked the ground, talked to old-timers, dug into records, some now lost forever, and told the tales that excited one's interest in the long-dead subject in the first place.

I am deeply appreciative of the contribution to this rendition of the John Larn story by those forerunners who cut this strange man's trail in earlier works:

Those correspondents at the town of Fort Griffin who, because Shackelford County was without a newspaper during the John Larn years, provided contemporary accounts of the dramatic events there in letters to newspapers around the state: "Sigma" of the *Galveston Daily News,* "Lone Star" of the *Fort Worth Daily Democrat* and the *Fort Worth Weekly Democrat,* "Comanche Jim" of the *Dallas Daily Herald,* "Clear Fork" of the *Jacksboro Frontier Echo,* and Carl Schulz of the *San Antonio Daily Herald;*

Don H. Biggers, whose *Shackelford County Sketches*, published in Albany, Texas, in 1908, was the earliest account in book form of the region and John Larn's impact upon it;

Edgar Rye, who, as justice of the peace, coroner, and county attorney at Albany, the seat of Shackelford County, played a personal role in the Larn story, and in 1909 published *The Quirt and the Spur*, a sometimes fictional, but nonetheless invaluable account of the dramatic events of those days;

Henry Griswold Comstock, eyewitness to the crimes Larn committed during his 1871 cattle drive to Colorado, whose narrative of that episode, first revealed in 1935, is the only known source;

Sallie Reynolds Matthews, a sister-in-law of John Larn, whose book *Interwoven: A Pioneer Chronicle* has been a rich source of information on the history of the Reynolds and Matthews families and the Clear Fork country since its publication in 1936;

Benjamin Ottis Grant, author of "An Early History of Shackelford County," a 1934 Master's thesis and the first scholarly study of the region's violent history;

John Chadbourne Irwin, an early resident of the Clear Fork country and a victim of Larn's criminality, whose recollections, written in the 1930s, provide a singular persective on the events of the time and the character of the man;

James Richard Webb, who interviewed many pioneers of Shackelford County in the 1940s and whose collection of documents concerning early county history has proved a gold mine for researchers;

Dr. Charles Leland Sonnichsen, whose account of Shackelford County violence in his book *I'll Die Before I'll Run: The Story of the Great Feuds of Texas*, based on research and interviews he conducted there in the 1940s, was published in 1962 and provided the general reading public its first glimpse of Shackelford County's violent past;

J. Evetts Haley and Hervey E. Chesley, who traveled the West in the 1930s and '40s, recording interviews with old-timers, some of whom had been at Fort Griffin during John Larn's day;

Carl Coke Rister, whose book *Fort Griffin on the Texas Frontier*, published in 1956, was the first full-length history of the short-lived military establishment on the Clear Fork of the Brazos;

Leon Claire Metz, prolific author of the West whose first book, *John Selman: Texas Gunfighter*, published in 1966, contained an abundance of previously unknown information on John Larn;

Frances Mayhugh Holden, who, in her *Lambshead Before Interwoven: A Texas Range Chronicle, 1848–1878*, published in 1982, included much of the Larn story;

Charles M. Robinson III, whose 1992 book, *The Frontier World of Fort Griffin*, was the first to focus on the history of the town that sprang up in the shadow of the fort by the same name;

Joseph Edwin Blanton and Watt Reynolds Matthews, members of the "interwoven" Reynolds and Matthews families of the Clear Fork, whose monograph *John Larn*, privately published in 1994, was the first publication devoted to the life of the controversial character;

And Ty Cashion, whose 1996 book, *A Texas Frontier: The Clear Fork Country and Fort Griffin, 1849–1887*, is the most scholarly, thoughtful treatment of the region's history to date.

In addition to their valuable published work, some of these researchers and writers, especially the late Dr. C. L. Sonnichsen, Leon Metz, Charles Robinson, and Ty Cashion, have been personally helpful to me and supportive of my work, and I want to express my sincere gratitude. Heartfelt appreciation is also extended to Margaret Putnam, current resident of the Larn home, who graciously welcomed my wife and me into it; Julia Putnam of Mineral Wells, Texas, who generously provided copies of Larn materials she had collected over many years; Mary Vandeventer of Lueders, Texas, who, with Julia Putnam, gave my wife and me a grand tour of the Larn home and ranch; Joan Farmer of Albany, Texas, who guided me through the historical files of the Old Jail Art Center in Albany and offered much insight into the Larn period; and to the following people who contributed in some way to this book: Diron L.

Ahlquist, Oklahoma City, Oklahoma; Jim Bradshaw, Nita Stewart Haley Memorial Library, Midland, Texas; Jennifer Bosley, Colorado Historical Society, Denver, Colorado; Carol Brooks, Arizona Historical Society, Yuma, Arizona; the late Jim Browning, Douglasville, Georgia; Donaly E. Brice, Texas State Archives, Austin, Texas; Betty Bustos, Panhandle-Plains Historical Museum, Canyon, Texas; Shirley and Clifton Caldwell, Albany, Texas; Lawrence Clayton, Abilene, Texas; Jerry Eckhart, Eastland, Texas; Gary Fitterer, Kirkland, Washington; Bob Green, Albany, Texas; Jan Hart, Irving, Texas; Allen Hatley, La Grange, Texas; Janice McCravy, Douglasville, Georgia; Ann M. Massman, University Library, University of Texas at El Paso; Rick Miller, Killeen, Texas; Chuck Parsons, Luling, Texas; Margaret Waring, Comanche, Texas; Ron Van Raalte, Roselle, Illinois.

Bravo of the Brazos

Introduction

"I believe that if a man was to shoot me through the heart I would kill that man before I died."

JOHN LARN

In the history of frontier violence in the American Southwest there is no stranger story than that of a man named John M. Larn, who, for a few brief years in the 1870s was at the very center of one of the most bitter, most deadly turmoils in Texas. The short, violent career of John Larn is a part of the story of the pioneer cattle industry that developed after the Civil War in the chain of counties stretching across north-central Texas. Larn's career peaked during the seventies, a turbulent time when Indian raids led to a major border war, outlawry and vigilantism flourished, and ranch fortunes were sometimes acquired by means of theft, treachery, and murder.

Outside of a few counties in northern Texas, John Larn is forgotten today, but he is well remembered in the Clear Fork county of the Brazos River where, nearly a century and a quarter after his death, the very mention of his name can trigger an instant and often acrimonious response. A western writer, who in the 1990s was researching the history of Shackelford County, interviewed a number of long-time residents. When he mentioned John Larn to one, the reaction was quick and crystal clear. "Leave Larn alone or I will kill you," the old-timer snapped, and the writer had no doubt he meant exactly what he said.[1]

Another author and researcher has recently remarked, "It says something about John Larn's character that, having been dead since 1878, he is still reaching out of his grave to hurt people."[2]

Researchers of the stormy history of the Clear Fork country, and especially Larn's role in that history, have met similar reactions from local residents. Dr. C. L. Sonnichsen, who delved into the record in the 1940s, found that few old-timers cared to talk about it "because it was painful to so many good people."[3] J. R. Webb, a Shackelford County researcher, in 1947 called the Larn story a "closed book." Students of the region's history, he said, had "been handicapped for the reason that most of the settlers feared they would go into the Larn affair and to this day they do not want to be quoted. A halo has been thrown around Larn's name by those residents who do not know the facts and by those who desire to glamorize the outlaw's deeds."[4]

In the 1960s author Leon Metz, while researching the Clear Fork activities of Larn's longtime friend and business associate John Selman, found that many citizens of the region refused to talk about Larn and that "practically every reference to him has been obliterated from the printed record. Larn is a memory all would rather forget."[5]

During his search Metz discovered a picture, a metal engraving on a block of wood, owned by a preacher in Roby, Texas, that was said to be an image of John Larn. It is the only known picture of the man. Metz had to run the engraving through a printing press to get a copy.[6] Thought to be a daguerreotype made in 1878,[7] it shows a dark-haired and dark-eyed man of good features, sporting a well-trimmed mustache and goatee. The bronzed lower face and white forehead immediately mark him as an outdoorsman.

There is something vague and mysterious about the man pictured, which is entirely appropriate, for John Larn was an enigmatic figure in his time, and mystery still surrounds him. Much of this is due to the manifest contradictions of his character. A successful cattle rancher, frontier sheriff of renown, architect of demonstrated talent, and loving husband and father, Larn was well-mannered and courteous around women and never drank liquor, used tobacco, or swore in their presence. He was undoubtedly a charismatic character, respected by men and admired by women. A contemporary newspaper described him as "fine looking, of good address, good nerve and a splendid marksman. On account of these traits he soon became popular on the frontier."[8]

And yet Larn was avaricious and greedy, an unscrupulous thief and cold-blooded murderer who, before reaching the age of thirty, killed or participated in the killing of at least a dozen men. He finally became so bold in his criminality that a mob of relatives and former friends and associates turned on him and brought his murderous career to a bloody end.

Edgar Rye, who, as justice of the peace for Shackelford County was in a position to know, wrote that during the first six months of Larn's term as sheriff of the county he "did more to quell lawlessness than any man . . . before or since his time."[9] Larn was, said Rye, "a careful, experienced cow puncher [of] exemplary conduct and clean personal habits, . . . unusually bright and intelligent."[10] But he was also "a veritable 'Dr. Jekyll and Mr. Hyde' [who] took part in some of the most fiendish acts of cruelty in those lawless days."[11]

Thirty years after Larn's death, newspaperman and historian Don H. Biggers interviewed many of the Shackelford County people who had known him, and concluded that he was "a mysterious and remarkable sort of a man [who] seemed to have many ambitions, . . . He was a man of attractive personality, more than average education and of pleasing address, . . . one of the most unique characters the West has ever produced, a man whose virtues his enemies praise and whose faults his friends admit and condemn."[12]

Sallie Ann Reynolds Matthews, John Larn's sister-in-law, told family members she remembered him as "young, handsome, dashing, and with manners that could never be offensive to a lady." She thought him "the very model of a gentleman. Shunning alcohol, tobacco and cursing, he stood in conspicuous contrast to the average frontiersman."[13] But, significantly, in *Interwoven,* her celebrated history of the Reynolds and Matthews families, who were her pioneer ranching kinfolk on the Clear Fork, Sallie Matthews never once mentioned Larn.

Watt Matthews, Sallie's son and Larn's nephew, summed up the man's complex character in plain language: "He was a charmer with many attributes of a gentleman, but he was an outlaw, a cow thief, and a killer."[14]

John Selman biographer Leon Metz described Larn as "one of the most plausible, unscrupulous and deadly characters who ever appeared on the Southwestern frontier."[15]

After years of studying the region, historian Rupert N. Richardson succinctly expressed his contempt for the man: "John Larn was morally dead."[16]

Larn was a shadowy figure in his time, and mystery still surrounds his memory. Even his name has confounded many. It has been recorded as "Larne," "Lorn," "Laren," "Lauren," "Laurens," and "Lawrence." Little is known of his early life prior to 1870 when, at the age of twenty-one, he seems to have settled permanently in the Clear Fork country. He told his wife he was born March 1, 1849, in Alabama and christened John M. Larn.[17] That is the way his signature, written in a clear and firm hand, appears on many documents in the Shackelford and Throckmorton County court records.

It appears from federal census records that the man known as John Larn in Texas was born in Georgia, raised in Alabama, and

that his name was actually "Laren." A federal census taker in Calhoun County, Alabama, on June 5, 1860, enumerated the family of
George A. Laren, a farmer from Missouri, and his wife, Elizabeth,
from Georgia. The Larens had eight children, ranging in age from
three to eighteen. The six oldest children, including John, the fifth,
were born in Georgia, the youngest two in Alabama. John Laren's
age was listed as twelve, a discrepancy of a year from the March 1,
1849, birth date provided by Larn, but census records, especially
early ones, are notorious for minor errors of this kind.[18]

Some Shackelford County residents recalled Larn saying he had
been raised in Atlanta, Alabama,[19] but there is no Atlanta in Alabama. The town he mentioned was probably Anniston, the county seat of Calhoun County. He told others he ran away from home
as a boy, went to Mobile, and worked as a "butcher boy," peddling
newspapers on trains.[20] As a teenager he became a cowboy and
drifted into the Clear Fork of the Brazos country, west of Fort
Worth, Texas, where in the 1860s Joseph Beck Matthews, Barber
Watkins Reynolds, John and William Hittson, and a few other
hardy pioneers had moved longhorn cattle onto free government
range land and established ranches. In 1867 and '68, Barber
Reynolds's sons drove herds from this area to Trinidad, Colorado,
following the trail blazed by Charles Goodnight and Oliver Loving
in 1866.[21] Young John Larn participated as a trail hand in at least
one of these drives.

In Colorado Larn took a job on a ranch at Patterson's Hollow,
some eighty miles northeast of Trinidad. According to the story he
later told Phin Reynolds in Texas, his employer neglected to pay
him, so he helped himself to one of the rancher's best horses and
rode out. The man caught up with him near Rocky Ford, bran-
dished a gun, and called out for him to halt. Larn whirled and, before the man could fire, jerked out his own pistol and shot him
dead.[22]

John Shanssey, a saloonkeeper at Fort Griffin on the Clear Fork,
and a man who had seen much of the frontier, told Reynolds a

slightly different story. Larn simply stole the horse, said Shanssey, and killed its owner when he was pursued.[23]

From Trinidad Larn rode down into New Mexico, where, as he later boasted, he killed an officer who tried to arrest him. Henry Griswold Comstock, who cowboyed with Larn in 1871, remembered him telling the story:

> I heard Laren describe the event; he said that he was standing at the door of a hurdy gurdy house . . . when the sheriff punched the muzzle of a cocked six shooter against his breast and said, 'Your name is Laren, I believe. You are my prisoner!' Laren said that he, with no show of excitement, stretched his neck as if looking at something going on back of the sheriff and that the sheriff turned his glance for an instant. He, Laren, drew and killed the sheriff in that instant. After telling that, Laren said, 'I believe that if a man was to shoot me through the heart I would kill that man before I died.[24]

Neither of these early killings has been substantiated—we have only Larn's word that they ever happened—but quick and deadly response to any challenge was fully consistent with the character of the man, as later events would prove conclusively.

In the spring of 1870 John Larn, twenty-one years old, was back on the ranges of the Clear Fork, working for the Reynolds and Matthews outfits. He boarded in the Stephens County home of Susan Reynolds Newcomb, the daughter of Barber Reynolds and recently widowed wife of schoolteacher Sam P. Newcomb. Also staying in the Newcomb home was nineteen-year-old Ben Reynolds, Susan's brother.[25]

By the following year, Larn's story would become more turbulent as his eight-year career on the Clear Fork began.

CHAPTER ONE

1871: Murder on the Trail to Colorado

"If I begin shooting, you all shoot too. And if they get the best of us and get me, you who escape make [it] back to Castle Gap and don't let any of them get through that Gap alive."

John Larn

In the summer of 1871 John Larn was working for a cattleman named William J. "Bill" Hayes, rounding up cattle in the country surrounding Fort Griffin in unorganized Shackelford County, Texas. Fort Griffin was a military post established in 1867 by the U.S. Army on the Clear Fork of the Brazos River. The fort provided the widely scattered settlers of Shackelford and surrounding counties with protection from raids by renegade Indian parties.

When the cattle roundup was completed, Hayes planned to deliver his herd to markets in Colorado. He had chosen John Larn to boss the roundup and trail drive. Although only twenty-two years old, Larn was an experienced drover, having already trailed to Colorado. To Hayes it was plain the young man possessed unusual leadership ability and skill in the handling of both wild cattle and tough men.

From the Fort Griffin country, Larn and his cowboys would follow the trail blazed by Goodnight and Loving in 1866. Fearing raids on the herd by fierce Comanche and Kiowa warriors who still freely roamed the Texas panhandle, Goodnight and Loving had not taken a direct, northwest route to Colorado, but chose instead a roundabout trail heading southwest. The trail followed the old rutted road of the Butterfield Overland Mail coaches, passed Fort Phantom Hill and Buffalo Gap, led on to Fort Chadbourne, and crossed the North Concho River to the Middle Concho. It followed the course of this stream into the parched wilderness called the Llano Estacado, the Staked Plains, the most arduous section of the trail for both men and beasts. On the other side of the Llano Estacado the trail entered the Castle Mountains and led through Castle Gap to Horsehead Crossing, the famous ford of the Rio Pecos, where the bleached skulls of hundreds of horses served as mute evidence of the toxicity of the alkaline pools on the river's flood plain. After following the Pecos to Pope's Crossing near the New Mexico line, Goodnight and Loving abandoned the old Butterfield Trail and then drove north up the river valley to Fort Sumner and on into Colorado through Raton Pass.

In the five years since Goodnight and Loving had first blazed this trail, the two partners and other Texas cattlemen had followed it each season with herds of Texas longhorns. The Reynolds brothers, George and Ben, with John Larn as one of their trail hands, traversed it several times. The threat of Indian attack was always present—Oliver Loving died of wounds received in a famous fight with Comanches on this trail in 1867—but for the most part hostile Indians avoided the desolate land. Nature's obstacles—the seemingly endless expanse of arid plain, the sudden wind storms, the poisonous water holes, the omnipresent stinging scorpions and venomous snakes—mainly plagued the drovers. The Goodnight-Loving or Pecos Trail, as it came to be called, was a killer road for both human and animal, and when John Larn went up that trail in 1871, he left more than the bones of alkali-poisoned horses along his path.

For the roundup and drive, Hayes hired a dozen young cowboys, a curious mixture of hardened desperado types and inexperienced range greenhorns. He knew little about John Larn, his foreman, other than that he was highly regarded by the Reynolds and Matthews boys and other cattlemen of the area, that he had been over the trail, was an expert with cattle and horses, and commanded respect from even the toughest die-hard cowboys. No doubt he had heard the stories of Larn's scrapes with the law, that he had killed a man or two, and that he was possibly using an alias. But on the Texas frontier in those days it was not considered polite—or healthy—to inquire too closely into a man's past, and Bill Hayes, who himself had little regard for the niceties of the law, may actually have been pleased to have a foreman with a shady past.

Larn's right-hand man was a fellow calling himself Bill Bush, although his real name was Delbert C. Clement.[1] Bush was a self-proclaimed desperado and killer. He told his fellow cowboys that following the ambush murder of his father at Sherman, Texas, he had left his home, his twin sister, and widowed mother to seek revenge. Proudly displaying a pistol with one notch cut in the handle, he bragged that he had already found and dispatched one of his father's killers. He fully expected to die with his boots on, he said, and didn't care how soon.[2]

Frank Freeman, Bill Hill, and Tom Atwell were other toughs believed to have dark histories, but they were much more closemouthed about their pasts. Freeman was the oldest of the hands, the only one with whiskers.

There were three unrelated cowboys named Wilson on the drive: Charlie, Billie, and Jim. Little is known of Billie and Jim, but Charlie Wilson was one of a family of brothers who in 1860 came from White River, Washington County, Arkansas, to settle near Graford, on Keechi Creek in Palo Pinto County, Texas. The oldest boy, William J., lost his right arm in a threshing machine accident and was known thereafter as "One-Arm Bill." His handicap did not prevent him from gaining widespread renown on the Texas frontier as a skilled drover and intrepid Indian-fighter. It was One-Arm Bill who, with a badly wounded Oliver Loving, held off a band of Comanches in a fierce battle in 1867. Loving later died and Wilson barely escaped with his life.[3] Younger Wilson brothers were Charlie, George, and Fayette. All became cattle drovers, gunmen, and occasional fugitives from the law. "It is not of record under what ill stars the Wilsons were born," Charles Goodnight said, "but it is a matter of tradition that they were born for trouble, and they never belied their birthright."[4]

All four Wilson boys were veterans of the Pecos Trail. One-Arm Bill and Charlie had ridden for Goodnight and Loving on that historic drive of 1866. They, along with brothers George and Fayette, had gone back over the trail several times since, working for Goodnight, John Hittson, and other cattlemen of the upper Brazos area.

Among the Hayes drovers was a young man named Font L. Twombly, who stood out in sharp contrast to most of the others. A member of a refined and well-to-do Detroit family, Twombly "carried the looks of refinement, rather delicate in appearance and very quiet and reserved in manner." Athletic and proud of his racing ability, he claimed he could cover one hundred yards in under ten seconds and said he would bet everything he had in a challenge race against any man in the world.[5]

Other Hayes hands included John Pettigrew, Missourian Albert Shappell, and twenty-year-old Henry Griswold Comstock. With his brother James, Henry Comstock had left his Wisconsin farm home after the death of his father in February 1871. The Comstock boys headed for Texas where they thought a cowboy career "would be like life in a rocking chair in the shade of great live oak trees."[6] At Fort Worth they were approached by One-Arm Bill, who was hiring hands for Bill Hayes. He offered them that job in the saddle they sought. They would be paid forty dollars a month to work the roundup, and, if they helped drive the herd to Colorado, they would receive an additional forty dollars to cover return expenses.

The Comstock brothers signed on and helped in the Hayes roundup. But before the drive began James fell ill and had to remain at Fort Griffin. Henry made the drive and later recorded his memories in a vivid account of that trip and the way it was managed by the foreman, John Larn.[7]

Early in September Larn's cowboys had assembled near Fort Griffin a herd of about 1,700 cattle, a mixed bunch of steers, bulls, cows, and calves gathered from Shackelford and surrounding counties. Hayes and Larn counted the herd and "went through the motions," as Comstock put it, of tallying the brands to determine ownership. Hayes said he recorded his tally at the county seats so that the owners could claim payment after the herd was sold in Colorado. Comstock believed him at the time, but, based on subsequent

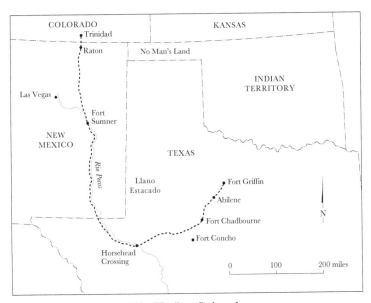

The Trail to Colorado

observation of the methods employed by Hayes and Larn, later changed his mind.

The drive started on September 10. Larn led them out in a southwestern direction, toward Fort Concho, where the herd was supposed to be inspected by a state official. Larn and Bill Bush rode on either point, directing the herd. When Larn scouted ahead, searching for water holes, good grass, and suitable bedding grounds, Charlie Wilson, another experienced drover, took his point position. Frank Freeman and Bill Hill had the swing positions close to the front. Flankers followed on either side. The greenest hands, including Henry Comstock, were always at drag, bringing up the rear, managing the horse remuda, chousing stragglers, and eating dust. John Pettigrew followed a few miles back with the chuck wagon.

Each man had three horses—one for morning, another for afternoon, and one for night guard. Comstock said that although the men at the point and sides had to be mounted, he and those in the drag walked much of the time in order to save their horses. They turned the ponies loose and let them trail along, saddled and bridled, ready for use if needed.[8]

As they neared Fort Concho, Larn turned the herd off to the west of the trail, explaining that he was in search of better grass, but the next day he said the drive was lost. He led them on west and a day or two later struck the trail on the Middle Concho River. Far back to the east lay Fort Concho, where the herd was to be inspected, but Larn assured the men they certainly would not go back. Although Larn made the avoidance of inspection sound perfectly innocent, it was at this point Comstock began to suspect the honesty of his foreman.

At the head of the Middle Concho they rested the herd and horses and let them drink their fill, for they were now entering Centralia Draw and the dreaded Llano Estacado, the toughest part of the drive. Ahead lay a stretch of nearly a hundred miles without the promise of water. For Comstock and the other greenhorns in the drag, it was particularly difficult. "The alkali dust was very bad," he said, "and I don't want to be as thirsty ever again as I was on some of those days."[9]

Finally the Castle Mountains loomed ahead. As the herd strung out to enter the narrow, boulder-strewn Castle Gap, Larn and Bush rode ahead to Horsehead Crossing, twelve miles beyond. Bush returned with canteens of water for the drovers. There was no holding the cattle when they smelled the water of the river; they broke and ran. The parched animals poured into the Pecos, those behind forcing the leaders across and up the other bank, where they turned, drove back to the water, and milled, drinking their fill.

Larn rested the herd for a day at Horsehead Crossing. Here Comstock spotted the dorsal fin of a fish in the muddy water. From the campsite of an earlier party he retrieved a heavy chalk line with a crudely made hook fashioned from the bale of a water pail. Baiting the hook with a kidney of the yearling Pettigrew had butchered for their next meal, Comstock threw it into the river. "Instantly it was seized and I pulled out a catfish three feet long," he said. Comstock then baited his hook with the other kidney and his second fishing attempt produced an identical result. "Then I quit," he said, "but we had fish for supper and it was a pleasing change from beef, fried bread and coffee without milk or cream or sugar three times a day and every day."[10]

It was while they were resting at Horsehead Crossing that Comstock first witnessed the murderous side of John Larn. One day two Mexican riders approached from upriver. Stopping on the opposite side, they called across in Spanish. "It soon seemed that they could not understand us, nor we them, so they rode on downstream," said Comstock.

They were barely out of hearing when Laren said: "I believe we ought not let those fellows get away," and he was backed promptly by Bush and Freeman and Hill and some others, and soon they were saddling their best horses and fording the river. . . . By this time the Mexicans were out of sight, but when they saw that they were followed by horsemen on the run, they turned and came back to meet their pursuers [who] were merciless and without words began shooting. One Mexican fell dead with the first volley. The other ran to the riverbank, which was fifteen or more feet high and perpendicular, and dove in and swam under the water like a muskrat with the heartless American murderers shooting at him until he sank from sight. . . . They dragged [the body of] the one that died on land to the bluff and pushed it over into the river. They called it feeding the catfish.

Comstock and those who remained at the crossing did not actually witness these murders, but they heard the shooting, and the killers bragged of their exploit when they returned with the horses, saddles, and bridles of their victims. The double murders were apparently prompted by nothing more than racial hatred and a covetous desire for the Mexicans' few possessions.[11]

At dawn the next morning Larn started the herd north up the east side of the Pecos. About noon a cloud of dust became visible far to the rear. Larn sent Frank Freeman back to see who was following them. Returning that evening, Freeman reported that a detachment of twelve U.S. Army cavalrymen, led by a corporal, was behind them. They were black troopers, well mounted on grain-fed horses and armed with repeating Spencer carbines. The corporal told Freeman they were from Fort Concho and were scouting for stolen horses. Considering their distance from Fort Concho, Larn found the story implausible.

The next morning, when it became evident the soldiers were still on their trail, Larn concluded the detachment had been ordered to bring the herd back to Fort Concho for inspection. When the cowboys gathered at the chuckwagon for noon grub, he asked if any of them wanted to turn the herd around and drive back across the Llano Estacado. Of course, none of them did. In that case, Larn said, everyone should eat hearty. He continued:

Then see to it that your shooting irons are in good working order and saddle your best horse. They have made noon camp down by the river in that clump of chaparral. We may surprise them. We may catch them off their guard, but we will find out if they want us or not. You fellows watch me. Let me do the talking, and if I begin shooting, you all shoot too. And if they get the best of us and get me, you who escape make [it] back to Castle Gap and don't let any of them get through that Gap alive. If they get you and don't get me that is what I will do for you. And don't lose your nerve.[12]

Backed by his men with arms at the ready, Larn confronted the cavalrymen. The corporal quickly recognized the gravity of the situation. It was obvious to him that these men would fight. In Comstock's words, he "saw which side his bread was buttered on, denied wanting us, asked for some fresh meat, which Laren gave them gladly, and we all rode back to the cattle in different spirits, I assure you, from what had prevailed the hours previous." Months later they learned that the troopers had returned to Fort Concho and reported they had bested the Larn party in a battle but could not get the cattle back through Castle Gap and had let them scatter. "There has never been any doubt in my mind," said Comstock, "but that they were bluffed."[13]

Inevitably there were losses of animals on the drive. Sick and injured cattle that could not keep up were usually shot by one of the drag herders, but there were also other losses due to the strain of the long drive. One day Font Twombly rode too near the head of an angry and footsore longhorn bull. With a quick twist of his head, the bull swung his horns and ripped the bowels from Twombly's horse, just missing the rider's leg. The other cowboys emptied their six-shooters into the angry animal, and both bull and horse were left for the wolves and buzzards.

When the chuckwagon horses gave out it became necessary to put six old longhorn steers under yoke. That required some effort, as Comstock recalled. It "was much like getting a wild broncho under saddle for the first time, the details of which depending entirely upon the disposition of each individual animal."[14]

Some stock was lost as a result of the one stampede the drovers experienced. One evening at chow time a storm broke with lightning and drenching rain. A great clap of thunder started the cattle running. It was so dark the cowboys could only see the heads of their own horses when the lightning flashed. They had to locate the cattle by the sound of their beating hooves. The herd became so scattered that Larn passed the word to let the longhorns go until they could be rounded up in the morning. The night was Stygian black and no one knew how to get back to camp. The temperature had plummeted, and all hands spent the night walking their mounts in a circle to keep warm. Tom Atwell shivered so hard everyone could hear his teeth chatter. In the morning they located the camp a mile or two away, had breakfast, and by noon the herd was back on the trail. Inevitably, however, the stampede had produced losses in missing, dead, or injured animals.

Many young cows were slaughtered to feed the drovers, who lived for months almost exclusively on a diet of bread, coffee, and enormous quantities of beef. Comstock said they "killed a big calf, a yearling, or sometimes a mature animal once, twice, or three times every day" for food.[15]

Not only animals met death on that trail drive. In late October Bill Bush killed Billie Wilson. One of the least talkative of the dozen drovers, Wilson, according to Comstock,

> had gotten some whiskey from a passing trader, with the result that it loosened his tongue and caused indiscretion. He was standing on one side of the campfire and made some remark indicating that he was good in a tussle or a fight. Bush, on the opposite side of the fire, seemed to think the remark directed at him and replied that he didn't brag about himself in a fight, adding, "When I fight, I fight from the belt." To

which Wilson replied: "Star Weno!" (esta bueno), . . . implying all right, or that suits me, as he reached over and drew a
knife from the belt of the man standing nearest him, and
raised it in a threatening manner. . . .

Bush drew his pistol and fired. Wilson was struck in the chest
and fell to the ground screaming. A second bullet from Bush's
sixshooter was "the shot of mercy," and the screaming stopped.
"Laren and Bush, I guess, did not sleep at all that night," said Comstock. "At daylight there was a little mound of freshly dug earth four
inches high, two feet wide, and six feet long, and poor Wilson was
no doubt covered less than a foot from the surface. . . . The herd
moved on."[16]

After many weeks on the trail, tension was building among the
men. There was almost another killing the day following Wilson's
death. Bill Hill, like Billie Wilson, was originally from Ohio, and
seemed to take the young man's sudden death particularly hard. At
the noon stop he took exception to an offhand remark by Albert
Shappell about the dead cowboy. Jerking out his pistol, he fired at
Shappell from eight feet away, but missed. The other men jumped
between the two and prevented another killing. Larn kept Hill and
Shappell separated until tempers cooled.

About this time Larn and Bush "perpetrated another dastardly
murder," as Comstock put it. When they came upon a young Mexican tending a flock of sheep, they started after him. The shepherd
quickly leaped on his horse and galloped off. He was better mounted, as the Texans rode horses that had not been grain-fed in months
and were jaded from the long drive. But Larn and Bush pulled rifles from their scabbards and began shooting at the fleeing Mexican. A shot broke the leg of his horse, toppling him. Larn and Bush
killed both the man and his horse, and left the bodies where they
fell. Comstock said he could not imagine why they killed this inof-
fensive sheepherder. Other than the sheep, he had no possessions
of value, and the killers made no effort to do anything with the

flock.[17] This cold-blooded murder seems to have been motivated by nothing more than racial hatred.

As October drew to a close, Bill Hayes appeared one day. He was driving a wagon loaded with supplies and trailing ten or fifteen fresh horses. At the end of the roundup season in Texas, Hayes had gone by stages from Fort Griffin to Trinidad, Colorado, where he purchased the badly needed replacement animals and goods. He accompanied his employees on the remainder of the drive.

A few days after Hayes joined the drive, he and Larn counted the herd. The cowhands strung out the cattle and passed them between the owner and his foreman, who tallied more than seventeen hundred head. Despite losses incurred on the trail, the herd had not diminished in size, but actually had grown larger. Larn had directed his men to pick up every stray animal they came across and drive it into the herd. Brands and ear markings were to be ignored. Of the seventeen hundred head, Comstock doubted more than four hundred actually belonged to Hayes. "I think Hayes was quite well pleased with the result of that count," he said. "He knew about as well as Laren did, about how much of it was due to Laren's nerve and management."[18]

To "nerve and management" might be added complete absence of scruples.

It was now November and as the drovers neared the Colorado line they began to experience cold nights and some blustery snow. By mid-November they entered the Raton Mountains, thrusting abruptly upward from the rolling prairie. The drive crossed the divide into Colorado and camped on a flat ten-acre plateau located some eighteen or twenty miles from Trinidad. They were joined in a few days by Silas Hough and thirteen cowboys who had been following them with a herd of thirteen hundred head.[19]

That night a blizzard struck and cattle from both herds drifted with the wind. The Hayes and Hough cowboys sought shelter in the canyons where they built huge fires and spent a miserable night. In the morning they found that the combined stock of the two outfits, three thousand head of cattle and one hundred horses, had disappeared from the plateau. Wading through deep snow, the cowboys were able to recover their mounts, but the cattle were hopelessly scattered. After more snow fell, the herd owners decided to set up winter quarters right where they were, and to remain until spring, when the cattle could be rounded up and sold.

They put up the hands in the empty cabins of the old Taylor Brothers Ranch. Compared to the rigors of the trail the work was easy, as Comstock attested: "We slept all night in the cabins, ate two good meals every day, and simply rode our horses . . . along the ridges [of] the outer limits of the range, turning the cattle in toward a common center."[20] That center was the valley of the Purgatoire River, called the "Picket Wire" by the Texans.

Most found the work pleasant duty for their forty a month but also found—except for Bill Bush, the self-advertised desperado—that it became monotonous. Bush began hanging out in Trinidad. Being a lover of good horse flesh, he spent much of his time in Barney Hill's livery admiring the fine stable of horses, especially a chestnut sorrel Kentucky racer well known around town. One morning Bush walked into the livery and told Hill's stableman to saddle up the chestnut sorrel. The man laughed, saying Mr. Hill's racehorse was not for hire, but his laughter died in his throat when Bush stuck the muzzle of a cocked sixshooter in his face and told him to follow orders. The terrified man obeyed and Bush galloped out of town astride the racer.

At the Taylor Ranch he showed off his purloined steed to the other cowboys but hastily departed when a three-man posse approached. With irate liveryman Barney Hill, who was toting a sixteen-shot Winchester, came Las Animas County Sheriff Juan Cristobal Tafoya, carrying a double-barreled shotgun, and his deputy, Lou Kreeger, carrying an old-fashioned muzzle loading target rifle with telescopic sights.[21]

Hill confronted John Larn and demanded to know why, as Bush's boss, he did not take the horse away from the thief. Larn shrugged and with a crooked grin replied that he reckoned it was for the same reason the animal disappeared from the livery stable in the first place: no one wanted to tangle with Bill Bush and his big sixshooter.

The posse easily picked up Bush's trail into the mountains. He was riding slowly, teasing his pursuers. When they closed near enough for Deputy Sheriff Kreeger to step off his horse and line up a shot with his scoped rifle, Bush would fire a shot in their direction and then gallop off. The posse was at a distinct disadvantage, for they certainly did not want to hit the valuable horse, whereas Bush did not care what he hit. Finally, the possemen gave up and returned to Trinidad.

Bush appeared in camp that night. After a discussion with Larn, he decided to return the racehorse. He and several others rode into Trinidad the next day. Barney Hill got his horse back with a note from Bush, written for him by the educated Font Twombly, saying: "I have always loved a good horse. I have had a ride on a good horse and I am satisfied, but don't follow me. Look out!"[22]

As the year ended, Henry Comstock and some other cowboys grew anxious to move on and asked Bill Hayes for their back wages. Confident that he would soon dispose of his herd, Hayes borrowed six hundred dollars for thirty days at an exorbitant interest of 6 percent per month and paid off those who wanted to leave. Comstock was among the men who left. He later returned to Shackelford County after visiting his old home in Wisconsin.

Remaining with John Larn in the Trinidad area were Tom Atwell, Font Twombly, and Charlie Wilson. Charlie's brothers, One-Arm Bill, Fayette, and George, were also nearby. All would become involved in more violence in the year to come.

CHAPTER TWO

1872: Trinidad Shootout and the Hittson Raid

"A band of notorious horse thieves is now congregated at or near the mouth of the Rio Hondo. . . . The names of the principal men are 'Chuck,' Jonnie Laurens or Lawrence, Charlie Wilson, Thomas Rhodes, and Thomas Atwell."

U.S. ARMY LIEUTENANT SARTLE

On Friday, February 2, 1872, a party of cowboys from the Hayes and Hough camps rode into Trinidad for a spot of fun. John Larn was with the group, as were all four Wilson boys, One-Arm Bill, Charlie, Fayette, and George. Tom Atwell, a cowboy named Payne Mason, and another calling himself Font Parkinson also rode along. The latter was undoubtedly Font Twombly, who had taken what the drovers called a "road" name. They checked into the United States Hotel and then split up to seek the pleasures afforded by the little border town.

Trinidad was the seat of Las Animas County, established only five years before. In early 1872 the town was still four years from incorporation and was little more than a village with a scattering of rude jacales and rough wooden shacks. A few false-front stores and saloons dotted its main street, and residents could boast of a newspaper, *The Trinidad Enterprise*, and the United States Hotel. Most of the residents were Hispanic.

Because there was no municipal government, county officers were responsible for law enforcement—what little there was. The town had earned an unenviable reputation for violence following the so-called Trinidad War four years earlier, when Anglos and Hispanics—"gringos" and "greasers" as they were called—engaged in a weeklong series of pitched battles. Several were killed or injured, and peace was not restored until troops from Fort Lyon arrived.

Juan Cristobal Tafoya, sheriff of Las Animas County, represented the law in Trinidad, with assistance from deputies Lewis M. Kreeger and Joaquin Young, the sheriff's son-in-law. Tafoya, having settled there in 1859, was one of the first residents of the area. As a deputy under then-Sheriff Juan Gutierrez, he had displayed great courage in attempting to separate the factions and control the violence in the Trinidad War of 1867–68.

Accounts of what happened in Trinidad on the afternoon of February 2, 1872 conflict, but most agree that George Wilson was at the center of the trouble. He had entered the Exchange, a combination saloon and gambling house operated by a man named Arbor, to try his luck.[1] That luck was bad, and George, enraged, leaped to his feet, claiming he had been robbed. He stormed out of the gambling house and began looking for his friends.

With reinforcements, he returned to the Exchange and loudly threatened Arbor, who tried to mollify him by offering to return any money George had lost. But George Wilson would not cool down. He pulled and cocked his sixshooter, and announced loudly that he had been cheated and someone must die for it. Sheriff Tafoya then appeared and, with pistol in hand, tried to subdue the furious cowboy. Wilson aimed his weapon at Tafoya's head. With his free hand the sheriff grasped the barrel, but before he could push it aside, Wilson fired, inflicting a mortal wound. Tafoya gave a convulsive leap and staggered forward, his pistol going off without aim. So rapid was the whole affair that before he hit the ground, two more bullets were shot into him. Wild confusion ensued. The people in the saloon rushed pell-mell into the street, some crawling across it through the mud in their fear of the Texan's bullets.[2]

According to early newspaper accounts—later denied—George Wilson, in addition to killing Tafoya, shot and wounded four other Mexicans in the Exchange that day.[3] Others may have taken part in the shooting. A few days after the affair, Font Twombly, alias Parkinson, wrote Henry Comstock that Tom Atwell had killed the sheriff.[4] And a story published in 1912 attributed the murder to "a gang of horse thieves, killers and rustlers composed of the Wilson boys, George and Fayette, Johnny Larn, Payne Mason, Font Parkinson, and Tom Atwell." In this version, the Texas cowboys started a brawl in the place, and Sheriff Tafoya "rushed into the thick of the fray just in time to face a dozen guns in the hands of the rowdies. It was apparent in an instant that somebody stood in line to be killed and it was none other than black Juan Tafoya, who went down like a martyr. He was fearfully punctured and was dead in a minute while everybody else fled the accursed place like rats from a sinking ship."[5]

Excitement ran high in the streets after the shooting. Atwell ran to the hotel with an angry crowd behind him, while the other Texans, pursued by another band of shouting townsmen, headed for the livery stable and their horses.

Trinidad storekeeper Frank Bloom remembered being in conversation with a cowboy in front of his store when the Wilson brothers came running by with a swarm of twenty or so infuriated Mexicans in their wake. George had lost his hat in the melee and grabbed the cowboy's as he went by. The U.S. Livery Stable, the cowboys' destination, was on the other side of an arroyo, traversed by a footbridge. When the cowboys reached their horses on the other side, One-Arm Bill Wilson grabbed his Spencer rifle from its scabbard, threw it across his stub arm, and called to his pursuers:

"The first man that crosses that bridge is a dead one."[6] Deputy Sheriff Joaquin Young impetuously started across "that terrible Rubicon and was rushing to a certain death" when others dragged him back out of danger.[7]

Atwell had been captured and held at the hotel, but the other Texans, now mounted and armed with rifles, rode to the hotel and freed him. The cowboys rode out of town, headed for their camp. Hastily formed posses pursued them. According to an early report,[8] a man named Sefarino Mestes, a member of one posse, was shot and killed only a mile from town by the retreating cowboys, and later another pursuing Mexican was also slain. These stories were denied in subsequent dispatches. The *Colorado Chieftain*, quoting *The Trinidad Enterprise*, said that only Sheriff Tafoya was killed, but the newspaper still denounced the murder, with more than a little hyperbole, as "the most cold-blooded, brutal, cowardly affair of the kind ever perpetrated in the west."[9]

One posse followed the cowboys all the way back to their camp. But the fugitives were "powerfully protected" by the range hands of the combined outfits, and the posse returned to Trinidad without making an arrest.[10]

Fearing the incident would precipitate another racial war in Trinidad, federal authorities wasted no time in sending troops from Fort Union to preserve order, but tempers cooled after the cowboys left. Juan Tafoya was buried, and Wilford B. Witt, appointed to replace him as sheriff, deemed it unwise to pursue the matter.

Bill Hayes, who still had not found a buyer for his cattle, continued to borrow against the herd to pay his expenses. Spring was approaching and it would soon be roundup and branding time in Texas. Hayes had other stock ranging the Clear Fork country and was anxious to get someone back there to look out for his interests. According to Henry Comstock, Hayes then made the gravest mistake of his life; he gave John Larn his power of attorney and asked him to return to Shackelford County to take care of his cattle.[11] Whether Hayes trusted his trail boss to this extent is questionable, but Larn, in any event, appeared in no hurry to begin the long ride back. He stayed in New Mexico for several months, hiring out his gun to an embattled Texas cattleman.

In the early months of 1872, John Hittson, a Clear Fork rancher, launched a campaign in New Mexico against Mexican and Anglo traders who trafficked in cattle and horses that were stolen in Texas by Comanche Indians. Hittson estimated that as many as 100,000 head of cattle had been lost by Texas ranchers to these thieves, known as Comancheros.[12]

Armed with a letter of authorization from the Texas governor and the power of attorney for nearly two hundred Texas ranchers, which authorized him to claim any of their branded stock he found in New Mexico, Hittson began organizing a band of fighting men. He recruited a force of gunmen from the Denver area and led them south to New Mexico. His close friend and trail-driving partner, James E. Patterson, followed with another band. They joined forces at the Clifton House, a large hotel on the Santa Fe Trail twelve miles below Raton Pass. Thomas L. Stockton, another former Hittson partner, owned and operated the Clifton House, which was also known as the Red River Station. Stockton enlisted a third group of fighting men, including two notorious local gun hands, Robert Clay Allison and John "Chunk" Colbert. Among those upper Brazos stalwarts who signed on for Hittson's Raid—as it came to be called—were John Larn, the four Wilson brothers, and Tom Atwell. Enlisting also were two New Mexico residents who had formerly lived in the Clear Fork country, brothers John and Thomas Selman.

Parties of Hittson mercenaries began sweeping New Mexico Territory, rounding up cattle and horses belonging to Texas ranchers, and turning them over to herders. The animals were then driven to Colorado and sold. New Mexico civilian and military authorities in general looked favorably on Hittson's campaign, but during the early weeks there was consternation in some quarters. On March 5 a Lieutenant Sartle wrote the commanding officer at

John Hittson led an army of mercenaries that included John Larn in a sweep across New Mexico Territory to recover cattle stolen in Texas by Comanchero thieves.

Fort Stanton that a "band of notorious horse thieves is now congregated at or near the mouth of the Rio Hondo. . . . The names
of the principal men are 'Chuck' [Chunk Colbert], Jonnie Laurens
or Lawrence [John Larn], Charlie Wilson, Thomas Rhodes, and
Thomas Atwell."[13]

The Hittson raiders continued to operate throughout the spring
and summer of 1872, and, surprisingly, most of the campaign was
conducted without bloodshed. There were incidents of violence,
however. On July 13 Chunk Colbert and a party of Hittson raiders
recovered some stolen cattle near Cimarron and took two suspected thieves into custody. On the road to town both suspects were
shot and killed.[14]

Although a coroner's jury deemed the actions of the Hittson
men justifiable, after this and other deadly clashes New Mexico
newspapers grew critical of Hittson and he lost most of his local
support. His cowboy gunmen began to drift away and the great
Hittson Raid drew to a close. The campaign had achieved much
success, however. The Comancheros had been dealt a severe blow.
Thousands of stolen animals had been retrieved and either sold or
turned over to the hired gunmen in lieu of wages. Hittson is said to
have collected a quarter million dollars in sales, which he divided
with the original owners.[15]

Many of the tough characters who rode with Larn that winter
and spring in New Mexico went on to untimely ends. Two of the
Wilson brothers reportedly died violently. Conflicting reports place
George Wilson's death both in Arizona[16] and near Fort Griffin.[17]
Fayette Wilson, according to one sketchy newspaper account, was
killed in San Antonio, Texas.[18]

The later violent career of Frank Freeman, a participant in the
1871 trail drive with Larn, has been better documented. Freeman
remained in New Mexico, and a few years later contributed to the
increasing notoriety of that territory—particularly Lincoln County—for unbridled violence. In February 1876, in company with the
infamous outlaw Jessie Evans, he helped gun down three Mexicans

suspected of horse thievery near San Agustin. The following December he shot and crippled a black soldier in Lincoln's Wortley Hotel in a senseless display of brutal racism reminiscent of Larn's murderous attacks on Mexicans during the trail drive of 1871. In August 1877 he and Charlie Bowdre, pal of Billy the Kid, rampaged in Lincoln. Freeman shot and wounded a sergeant from Fort Stanton and rode up and down the street, firing his pistol and shouting that "his name was Frank Freeman and no twenty men could arrest him," that "he had his man for all meals in the day and . . . intended to kill every man in town that he didn't like." Sheriff William Brady and a posse finally corraled Freeman and Bowdre. When outraged citizens threatened to take the prisoners, Brady, with the help of a military escort, hustled them off to Fort Stanton. Freeman escaped from the fort, but a posse led by Sheriff Brady and augmented by a military detail trailed him to his hideout on the Rio Ruidoso and in a running gunfight shot him to death.[19]

On January 7, 1874, two Hittson Raid compadres, Chuck Colbert and Clay Allison, clashed in Tom Stockton's Clifton House, and Allison shot Colbert dead. Thirteen years later, on July 3, 1887, Allison was thrown from the wagon he was driving near Pecos, Texas, and killed.[20]

Shortly after it was reported that he had joined a band of horse thieves on the Rio Hondo, John Larn left New Mexico and Hittson's employment. Together with Tom Atwell, Payne Mason and Font Twombly, alias Parkinson, who had all participated in the Trinidad shootings, he headed back to the Clear Fork country. Still wishing to avoid the hostile Indian threat and unfamiliar trails and watering holes of the Texas panhandle, Larn chose to return by a different route. He and his cohorts rode east through southern Kansas and then south through Indian Territory toward Shackelford County.

At some point during the journey four other riders joined them. The newcomers, Thomas Alden, Norman Patterson, Alex Motley, and C. D. Merrill, were evidently as tough an outfit as the Larn party. On April 4 in Indian Territory, a unit of the 10th U.S. Cavalry arrested all eight "by order of Brevet Major General Benjamin H. Grierson," and threw them in the stockade at Fort Sill. Grierson, commanding the 10th Cavalry and the fort, had information that Mason and Twombly were wanted for murder and that Patterson was wanted for unspecified crimes in Colorado. A federal warrant was also issued for Merrill on charges of whiskey peddling. The military apparently shackled and jailed the other five on the mere grounds that they were suspicious characters traveling in bad company. After holding them two days the officers released Larn, Atwell, and Alden. Motley secured his freedom a few days later. A deputy U.S. marshal took charge of Merrill on April 21 and transported him to Fort Smith, Arkansas, where he would face the federal court. On May 3 military authorities turned Patterson over to the sheriff of Pueblo County, Colorado. When no civil authorities arrived to take charge of Mason and Twombly, the former was allowed to "escape guard" on May 8. Two weeks later, "by order of General Grierson," Twombly was released.[21]

After his release at Fort Sill, John Larn, accompanied by Atwell, rode on to Fort Griffin on the Brazos. There he was soon joined by John Selman, whom Larn had first met while riding for Hittson. Selman showed up in Texas driving a wagon and accompanied by his wife, two young sons, and his brother Tom. Selman had lived for several years in the Clear Fork country during the '60s, but that was before Larn came to the region. The Selmans had joined the Goodnight and Loving original 1866 drive to New Mexico and remained there. In 1872 Larn and John Selman became firm friends and business associates, and from that time until Larn's death six years later their names would be closely linked.

Many came to believe it was a partnership made in hell.

As both men were named John, folks began calling Selman "Old John" to distinguish him from Larn, who was ten years younger. The name stuck and Selman was called "Old John" the rest of his life.

John Selman hooked up with John Larn for the first time during the
Hittson Raid of 1872. Courtesy of the Western History Collections,
University of Oklahoma Library.

The association of John Larn and John Selman is one of the strangest in the history of the West. In 1872 Selman was thirty-three years old, a mature family man, a veteran of the frontier, and, by all accounts, a man of courage, integrity, determination, and resolve—one not easily influenced by others. During his years in the Clear Fork country he had twice served as sheriff of Stephens County,[22] and he was admired and respected by the Reynolds, Matthews, and Hittson families, the prominent ranchers of the region. In New Mexico, Lucien Maxwell, the prosperous Colfax County landowner, thought well enough of Selman to present him with a quarter section of land, totalling 160 acres, as a gift.[23]

The records do not link Selman's name to any kind of criminal activity prior to 1872. And yet, after teaming up with John Larn, a young fellow ten years his junior, Selman's life reversed itself completely. He became notorious throughout the West as one of the most unprincipled criminals and deadliest killers in the country, with the blood of at least twelve victims on his hands. As his biographer has pointed out, "Selman was subjected to powerful suggestions of evil from this man [Larn] who may have been one of the most plausible, unscrupulous and deadly characters who ever appeared on the southwestern frontier. . . . An even bigger enigma than Selman himself, . . . Larn may have been Selman's evil genius."[24]

When Larn died six years later, he was guilty of much more than his own crimes.

John Henry Selman was born in Madison County, Arkansas, on November 16, 1839. At the age of nineteen he moved with his family to Grayson County, Texas. By 1861 he was living in Stephens County, just east of Shackelford, where he served as sheriff for six months before enlisting in the 22nd Regiment, Texas Cavalry, on December 15 of that year. He was stationed at Fort Washita in the Choctaw Nation. His muster-roll card described him as twenty-two years of age, five feet, ten inches in height, with dark hair, dark complexion, and blue eyes.[25] Those deep-set eyes were such a pale blue that the iris was almost indistinguishable from the white, giving him a strange, unearthly look that is evident in photographs. He had a habitual hangdog manner and avoided looking people in the eye, which only increased the startling effect of his pale gaze when he looked up.[26] Several who knew Selman in those early days remarked on his eyes. Frank Collinson said they were very unusual, "such a light blue that it was hard to see where the blue began and the white stopped."[27] The pallor of Selman's eyes caused John P. Meadows to believe they were gray, not blue. Through bitter experience Meadows came to have an utter contempt for Selman, whom he described as having "cold gray eyes set deep back in his head, large mouth, and no soul whatever."[28]

Selman twice walked away from the Confederate Army. The first offense was treated as a simple case of absence without leave, but when he disappeared again on April 25, 1863, never to return, he was charged with desertion. Folks on the Clear Fork were well aware that Selman was a deserter but did not condemn him. On the contrary, they seemed to have admired him for leaving an unimportant military post to care for his widowed mother, three sisters, and fourteen-year-old brother, Tom.

Like John Larn, Thomas Selman, nicknamed "Tom Cat," was born in 1849; unlike Larn, Tom was a follower, not a leader, and always remained in the shadow of his older brother. Physically, he was not as robust as "Old John," and has been described as "small-boned and in shaky health."[29]

At Fort Davis—a clutch of picket cabins erected in Stephens County, Texas, as a civilian outpost to defend against Indian raids—John Selman joined the state militia and was elected lieutenant. In August 1865 he returned to Grayson County, Texas, to marry Edna DeGraffenreid, an eighteen-year-old girl who was also from Arkansas, and took his bride back to Fort Davis. In January 1866 he again accepted appointment as sheriff of Stephens County,[30] but when Goodnight and Loving rounded up their cattle and prepared to blaze the trail to Colorado, Selman decided to go along. With his wife Edna and brother Tom, he drove a wagon behind the herd.

The Selmans started a ranch in Colfax County, New Mexico, and Edna gave birth to two boys, Henry in 1869 and William in 1870. But the Indians drove off all their stock and times were rough. John was hard pressed to put food on the table for his growing family. In 1872 he welcomed the opportunity to make a few dollars as a gunman in the Hittson Raid. Impressed by another Hittson mercenary, the charismatic John Larn, Selman decided to return to the Clear Fork country and join Larn in his ambitious cattle ranching plans. On his return to Texas he filed on a 160-acre homestead on Tecumseh Creek in Throckmorton County, just north of Shackelford, and began construction of a one-room picket house. He later moved from this original dwelling to a stone building on the other side of the creek. The new house was called "Rock Ranch." He had a few head of cattle that he threw in with Larn's small herd, and the two men became ranching partners.[31]

John Larn was also contemplating house and home. All during his months in New Mexico he had been thinking of Mary Jane, the pretty fifteen-year-old daughter of Joe Matthews. Not long after his return to Shackleford County, he proposed marriage.

The women of the Matthews and Reynolds families were taken with the darkly handsome Larn. There is no question he could charm the ladies. Sallie Ann Reynolds, who would marry Mary Jane's brother, said Larn was "the sort of man who could sweep a young lady off her feet."[32] Larn did not drink, smoke, chew tobacco, or curse in the presence of his wife or any other lady, but, as Selman's biographer has pointed out, he did not commit any murders in their presence either.[33]

Some men of the Reynolds and Matthews clans, having heard stories of Larn's criminal history, opposed the marriage. When Barber Reynolds, father of Sallie Ann and patriarch of the Reynolds family, learned of the betrothal, he rode a hundred miles from Weatherford, Texas, to advise Joe Matthews against allowing it.[34] But Mary Jane, "a pretty brunette with curly brown hair, large blue eyes, a lovely figure, and a strong will,"[35] was in love and determined.

Mary Jane Matthews was charmed by the courtly manners of the darkly handsome John Larn and married him in 1872. Courtesy of Julia
Putnam.

Plans for the wedding proceeded despite the warnings. On November 28, 1872, John Larn and Mary Jane Matthews were joined in matrimony.[36]

Larn built a small cottage on the north bank of the Clear Fork near the site of a deserted army post called Camp Cooper, where a U.S. Army colonel named Robert E. Lee had held command in 1856 and '57. Using the stones of the fort's storage buildings and assistant surgeon's quarters, he built his three-room cottage. He even laid out a small formal garden that hinted at a love for cards. The shapes of the four playing card suits were outlined with stones and then enclosed in rock-bordered rectangles. The place became known as the "Honeymoon Cottage," and is still called that over a hundred years later.[37]

There is no doubt Mary Jane was devoted to her husband; she stood by him throughout their turbulent six-year marriage and defended his memory until the day she died. Larn apparently had a deep affection for his young wife—nothing in their marital history indicates otherwise—and marriage into the influential Matthews family was unquestionably a giant step forward for the ambitious young man. The five hundred head of cattle Joe Matthews gave Larn as a wedding present was one of the first benefits he enjoyed.[38] By the age of twenty-three he was well on his way to becoming a prosperous cattleman.

The "Honeymoon Cottage," the first home of John and Mary Jane Larn. The borders of its formal garden are still visible. Courtesy of Julia Putnam.

Joseph B. Matthews gave his daughter and her husband five hundred head of cattle as a wedding present.

CHAPTER THREE

1873: The Bush Knob Massacre

"I heard Laren say many times that dead men tell no tales."

HENRY GRISWOLD COMSTOCK

In May 1873 four cattlemen brothers, Emmett, John, Dick, and Creed Roberts, moved their herd west from the range in Stephens County through Shackelford to new grazing land in Jones County. This was John Larn country, and in 1923, half a century later, Emmett Roberts remembered vividly what he called "an interesting experience with John Laurens, a 'bad man' of that day and a cattle thief." Of course "Laurens" was John Larn, who was working cattle in the southern sections of Shackelford County that spring. Larn and his men were supposedly rounding up and branding calves that followed his own cows, but, as Roberts's story affirms, Larn was not averse to changing brands on other cows he found. "He would 'burn out' the brands," said Roberts,

and brand them with his own brand, and also mark them. But my brand, JPB with the B lying against the other two letters, was hard to burn out. Also, as it happened, part of the cows he had branded out of my herd were old gentle milk cows, and I knew them anyway. Laurens was not with the herd when I came up, but a fellow named Wilson was watching the

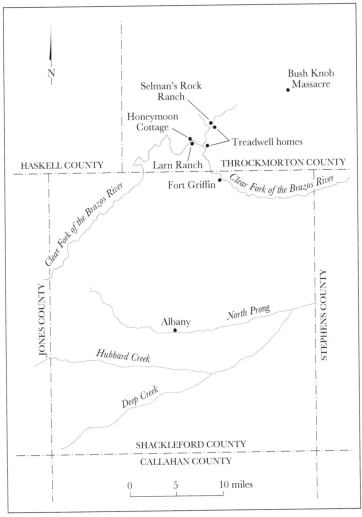

John Larn Country

herd.[1] I rode up and told him that he had some of my cattle, and that I wanted to get them. He told me to go see Laurens, who was away about a half mile shoeing his horse. I insisted that I knew the cattle, and that I wanted to get my own stuff, that we didn't need Laurens. But Wilson insisted, and when I began to work the herd trying to cut out my cows, he began following me up trying to undo what I was doing, and protesting all the time that if I had any cattle in that herd to go get Laurens—he was the man who had branded them. But I continued, and as I glanced over my shoulder I thought I saw him raise his rifle as though fixing to fire. I had no chance to protect myself and work the cattle also (we were all heavily armed with pistol and Winchester, and Wilson was carrying his rifle across the pommel of his saddle), so I called in George Outlaw, who was with me, . . . and told him to cut the cattle out while I watched Wilson. Before this I had asked Wilson if he wanted to scrap me over the matter, and he said he did not, but that he wanted me to see Laurens before I cut out the cattle.

Other Larn cowboys rode up to find out what all the fuss was about. Outlaw, seeing that he and Roberts were greatly outnumbered and would have no show in a fight, refused to cut out the disputed cattle. This further enraged young Roberts, but he decided his only recourse was to find John Larn and argue his case. At Larn's camp he was greeted cordially and invited to join the cowboys at the chuck wagon for a meal. Larn agreed to return to the herd with Roberts and permit him to cut out any of his freshly branded cattle. Larn insisted, however, said Roberts,

that in order to determine this I would have to ride into the herd and rope and throw the cattle I claimed. I told him there was no sense in doing this, that I knew the cattle, that he knew them, and knew that he had lately burned out my brand and placed his own on them. He kept insisting, and I was just as determined that I was not going to do that, and told him to give the cattle up without further ado. I do not know where matters would have drifted to; it looked like a fight with odds against me.

Just at that critical moment eight horsemen appeared. They turned out to be riders for ranchers up in the Fort Belknap country led by Archie Medlin who were on the same mission as Roberts—to claim cattle Larn had illegally branded. "We had it on Laurens then, and he knew it," Roberts recalled with some satisfaction. "I set in and cut my cattle out, and asked Medlin if he needed any help with his. When he replied that he did not, I moved on."[2]

The full realization of how near he came to death that day must have struck Roberts seven months later when he heard about the Bush Knob Massacre, the most sanguinary deed in John Larn's murderous history.

At the roundup that spring Larn slapped his own brand on all cattle he could find that belonged to Bill Hayes, who was still back in Colorado trying to dispose of his trail herd. Hayes finally returned in the summer of '73 and was appalled to find that his Clear Fork range herd had disappeared, and was now integrated into Larn's own herd by the magic of the branding iron and perhaps the power of attorney Hayes is said to have given his former foreman. Financially ruined, Hayes was furious, but not so angry that he was ready to confront the man he knew to be an extremely dangerous gunman. He bided his time and waited for an opportunity to get even.

In the fall he thought he saw that opportunity. He negotiated a contract to deliver a herd of cattle to reservation agents at Fort Sill in Indian Territory and, with the help of his brother, John, began recruiting drovers. One of the first he hired was Bill Bush, the aspiring desperado who had been Larn's enthusiastic accomplice in his murders on the trail to Colorado and had gunned down poor Billie Wilson on that drive. Others who signed up with the Hayes brothers were John Webb, George Snow, Guy Jeames, "Doc" Hearn, and Webster Hazlett. Webb was an employee of Fort Griffin businessman Dennis Murphy and a close friend of James Comstock, Henry's brother. Jeames was nicknamed "Jesse James," and Doc Hearn was also called "Hard Times." Hazlett's name has also been given as "Haylet" and his first name as "John."[3]

In late November 1873, the Hayes brothers quietly gathered a herd, instructing their hands not to be too careful with regard to brands and definitely to throw in any animals carrying the Larn brand and markings. By the time the drive to Fort Sill was begun, the Hayes herd numbered over a thousand head.

When John Larn got wind of the move he immediately went to twenty-nine-year-old G. Riley Carter, a neighboring rancher. Carter had been deputized as a constable by Sheriff J. H. Caruthers of Palo Pinto County, to which Shackelford and Throckmorton Counties were attached at this time. Larn and Carter somehow secured a warrant for Bill Hayes's arrest on a rustling charge, though it is unclear what judicial authority authorized its issuance. At the head of a posse that included the Selman brothers and a cattle inspector named Beard, Larn and Carter called on Colonel G. P. Buell, commander at Fort Griffin, and requested the help of the military to pursue the Hayes outfit. Buell ordered 2nd Lt. Edward P. Turner, Troop D, 10th Cavalry, to lead a detachment and assist in the serving of the warrant. On December 3 the civilian posse and a detail of seventeen black troopers, the vaunted "buffalo soldiers," left Fort Griffin in pursuit of the Hayes outfit.[4]

The next morning the combined civilian and military posse approached an area in south-central Throckmorton County called Bush Knob after the creek running fifteen miles through it. A young cowboy named Drew Kirksey Taylor, riding line for the Browning brothers of Throckmorton County, caught sight of the posse as it topped a rise in the distance. "I was just a boy then, but I remember the incident quite clearly," Taylor wrote later.

[I] saw a party of men at a distance, and at first I was not sure whether they were Indians or white men. I stopped for a while and looked at them, and as they did not ride like Indians I decided they were soldiers. I then galloped my horse around a bunch of cattle I was driving, and was riding west, when suddenly they started in a run toward me. I then stopped and waited until they came up, and as they approached I heard one of them say, "Oh, that's just a boy." They rode up and one of them asked me if I knew of any cow outfit passing through or camped in that part of the country.

Taylor replied that as a matter of fact he had only that morning stopped at the camp of the Hayes brothers, who were resting a trail herd about six or seven miles away. He cheerfully gave directions to the spot. "They then left me," Taylor recalled. "I did not know then that I had given these inhuman brutes the information that led them to the camp where they brutally murdered unsuspecting and innocent men. These Negro soldiers, headed by two White outlaws, one by the name of John Laren, and the other named John Selman, . . . followed the direction I had given them and located the camp of the Hayes outfit."[5]

With Taylor's unwitting help, Larn and Turner were able to approach the Hayes camp stealthily. They had their men dismount some distance away and, using the banks of Bush Knob Creek as cover, follow the stream to the campsite. Four men, Bill and John Hayes, Bill Bush, and George Snow, were in camp eating their noon meal. Four others, Jeames, Hearn, Webb, and Hazlett, were minding the herd.

Reports of what then transpired are confusing and contradictory. Lieutenant Turner's official report to his superiors is the only known account by one who was on the scene. He said that the four men in camp, finally spotting the possemen skulking along the creek bank, grabbed their weapons and opened fire. In the answering rifle barrage, two were killed instantly and the other two were shot down as they tried to escape.[6]

According to an account appearing in *The Galveston Daily News*, the posse leaders initially attempted to place the four drovers under arrest. "Two of these men were arrested, and the other two resisted by firing their revolvers at the constable's party. At the time the firing commenced, the two who were in arrest attempted to escape, one of them grasping a carbine belonging to a member of the guard, and the four were instantly shot and killed."[7]

Drew Taylor, the young cowboy who always regretted directing the pursuers to the Hayes camp, said that the posse opened fire without warning, killing all four: "I was one of the men who helped to bury those unfortunate cowboys, and when I say it was diabolical murder I know whereof I speak."[8]

Henry Comstock believed his personal experience with the characters of many of the principals gave him special insight into what took place. "As I picture it, knowing the men as I knew them, I would say that Laren killed Bush first and Hayes next and possibly one or two of the others. Bush [was] known by Laren as the dangerous one and Hayes because he was in Laren's way."[9]

His bloody work accomplished at the camp, Larn led a party after the four other Hayes herders and arrested them. Larn's men then took charge of the herd and turned it back toward Shackelford County. In camp that night the rest of the Hayes outfit was killed. According to Lieutenant Turner's report, sentinels shot them down when they attempted to escape. This version is repeated in the *Galveston Daily News* account.[10]

Capt. Richard Henry Pratt, an officer at Fort Griffin during this time, remembered that the combined military and civilian force trailed "an organized gang [of] horse and cattle thieves [to] their rendezvous well out in the buffalo region," where two corrals, four miles apart, were found, with "five white men at one and four at the other and nearly a thousand cattle, and about forty horses between them." The posse captured both parties "without firing a gun

[but] during the night the prisoners . . . tried to get away and all were shot to death." It was the position of the civilian posse members, Pratt said, "that stock stealing along the border was so common that it was impossible to get a clean jury against it and the best way to end it was to end the thieves when caught."[11]

Eight men were dead at Bush Knob, and military and civilian officials shrugged. There were some, however, who considered the slayings to be cold-blooded murder. "Laren and Selman claimed that those cowboys made a fight and would not surrender, and that they had to kill them in self defense, which was not true," said Drew Taylor. "They did not give those cowboys a dog's chance."[12]

"There is no doubt in my mind," wrote Henry Comstock, "but that Laren killed the four prisoners, because I heard Laren say many times that dead men tell no tales." Comstock said that the saddles of the four men were burned, a good indication that they were shot in the head while sleeping cowboy fashion, with their heads on their saddles.[13]

Other newspaper accounts exploded the story into a wild tale of frontier warfare. The *Fort Worth Weekly Democrat*, for instance, reprinted an unverified report taken from a Weatherford paper of December 15 in which was described a gun battle at the "James' Ranche, on the Clear Fork of the Brazos, six miles below Fort Griffin." The place owned by "Old Man James" was said to be "surrounded by the worst set of desperadoes and cattle thieves" infesting the country. An enraged citizenry, supported by troops from Fort Griffin, rode out to break up the gang and drive its members away.

> Upon arriving at James' Ranche they were immediately fired upon by about twenty-five of the desperadoes, all armed to the hilt with Henry rifles and two six-shooters each. The detachment immediately charged the ranche, keeping up a hot fire all the time, and as the house was rather open, the bullets induced the outlaws to retreat. . . . As they left the house

[they] were shot down by the frontiersmen that accompanied the troops. . . . The killed are Wm. Hayes, Geo. Snow, "Doc" Hern, "Gov." James, John Webb, "Hardtimes," and Wm. Bush. The remainder of the party escaped; none seriously wounded except "old man James"—he was noticed to mount his horse with great difficulty. This virtually broke up the worst nest of desperadoes on the Texas frontier, and one that has been the cause of all the horrible murders that have been committed in the vicinity of Griffin for the past four years.[14]

Of course, there was no "James' Ranche" run by "Old Man James" in the vicinity of Fort Griffin. The youngster killed at Bush Knob, Guy Jeames (or "Gov." James in the Weatherford report), was, according to Drew Taylor, the son of a widow who lived near Fort Griffin. The specious story was spread by John Larn and his admirers to turn the incident from what it really was—a cold-blooded mass murder perpetrated in furtherance of Larn's avaricious ambitions—into a tale of heroism carried out for the benefit of the region.

Charlie Wilson, who had ridden with Larn on the Pecos Trail drive and had sided with him during the turbulent Trinidad and Hittson Raid episodes, barely escaped being the ninth victim in the Bush Knob Massacre, said Henry Comstock. Charlie, like Larn, married the daughter of a Clear Fork rancher. He had originally agreed to help Hayes take the herd to Fort Sill, but at the last minute decided to stay on a few more days with his bride and promised to catch up later. When Mrs. Charlie Wilson got news of the massacre, she realized how close she had come to early widowhood. She blamed the army for the atrocity. Said Comstock:

> While everybody for miles around was talking excitedly about it, Charlie's wife buckled on a six-shooter, mounted a pony, and rode up to the home of the officer in command at Griffin. . . . When [Colonel Buell] appeared at the door, she called

out in loud, clear tones: "I am Charlie Wilson's wife and I come to warn you that if you or any of your men touches a hair of my Charlie I will just blow the top of your head right off." Then she drew her gun, flourished it, fired a shot in the air, turned her pony, and cantered away.[15]

Charlie Wilson, much better acquainted than his feisty bride with the character of John Larn, must have known who really initiated the slaughter, but if he ever confronted Larn about the matter, it is not recorded.

After being driven back to the vicinity of Fort Griffin, the captured herd was held for inspection by ranchers who claimed Hayes had stolen from them.[16] It is certain that John Larn led the list of claimants. There was no attempt at an inquiry into the eight deaths at Bush Knob. As Drew Taylor said: "In that day and time there was not very much said and nothing done in the way of prosecution with regard to anyone found dead."[17]

Larn returned to his Honeymoon Cottage in time to be at his wife's side when she delivered their first child on December 17, 1873. They called the boy William Alexander Larn.

CHAPTER FOUR

1874: Early Fort Griffin and the Old Law Mob

"Bryant was killed by one of Larn's hands under circumstances to arouse the suspicions of the people that it was done to get his cattle. Larn kept the cattle without administration."

GALVESTON DAILY NEWS
July 13, 1878

John C. Jacobs, an early resident of Shackelford County, believed that the period from 1874 to 1880 at Fort Griffin and vicinity "was the toughest stretch of years any town ever experienced. There were more cold-blooded murders that went unnoticed and there were killings for which no trial was ever held."[1]

One of these killings occurred near Larn's Honeymoon Cottage in April 1874. When a man remembered only as "Bryant" showed up in the area with a few head of cattle, Larn welcomed him, permitted him to throw his cows in with the Larn herd, and even let him sleep in his house. According to the sketchy newspaper accounts, based entirely on Larn's version of events, Bryant and Tom Atwell, who was still working for Larn, had an argument on April 18 over the branding of a yearling. Larn tried to separate the two men, but Atwell pulled a gun and shot the unarmed Bryant, killing him. Larn said he attempted to arrest Atwell, and even fired two or three shots at him when he fled, but the killer made his escape.[2] It was later reported that "Bryant was killed by one of Larn's hands under circumstances to arouse the suspicions of the people that it was done to get his cattle. Larn kept the cattle without administration. Bryant had no relatives or friends who cared to investigate the matter."[3] Whether Larn had a hand in the killing is not known because Atwood disappeared from the area and no one was ever charged with the murder, but once again the cattle herd of John Larn had expanded at the cost of a man's violent death.

The year of 1874 was momentous for citizens on the Clear Fork. That was the year of the Red River War in which warriors of the Kiowa, Comanche, Southern Cheyenne, and Arapaho Indian tribes left their reservations in the Indian Nations and clashed with the U.S. Army on the plains of northern Texas. The problems Clear Fork residents had experienced for years with marauding Indians were only intensified when the tribes resorted to warfare.

John Larn had a narrow escape from Indians in February 1874, an adventure chronicled in several newspapers across the state. While searching for strayed horses near Flat Top Mountain, Larn saw horsemen approaching. Thinking they were members of a cavalry scouting detail from Fort Griffin that he knew to be in the vicinity, he rode toward them. Suddenly the party divided and moved to encircle him. Aware now that these were hostile Indians, he turned his horse and rode for his life. The newspapers reported that he was "closely pursued by 12 or 15 savage fiends yelling and shooting," but he was well mounted and by "expert riding" managed to escape. The Indians followed him almost to his home, but "obliqued right, going through the Matthews's field, taking his horses, then crossed the river, getting G. R. Carter's, John Newcomb's and John Selman's horses, getting, in all, nearly twenty head."[4]

Indians were not the only terror along the Clear Fork. John Selman and his family had a harrowing experience a few months later when a cougar attacked them in their home. The Selmans, alarmed by the frantic barking of their dog, opened the cabin door to discover the big cat. It sprang into the room and snatched up one of the children in its powerful jaws. A man named Hewitt, who lived with the Selmans and was described as "gifted with uncommon size and strength," siezed the animal with his bare hands and managed to free the child. Selman grabbed his rifle and pumped two shots into the beast, but it still showed signs of life. Hewitt dragged it out into the yard, where it finally died. From nose to tip of tail, the big cat measured eleven feet, nine inches in length.[5]

Depredations by both Indian and white stock thieves in the northern counties of Texas led the state legislature in the spring of 1874 to authorize formation of a Frontier Battalion of Texas Rangers under the command of Maj. John B. Jones. John Larn, like most of his Clear Fork neighbors, no doubt welcomed this news, but he could not foresee the important role that rangers of the Frontier Battalion would play in his future, a role not altogether to his liking.

Another decision of the Texas Legislature in 1874 significantly affected life on the Clear Fork. In the fall lawmakers responded favorably to petitions requesting permission to organize Shackelford County, which had remained unorganized since it had been carved from Bosque County in 1858 and named for Dr. John J. Shackelford, a hero of the Texas Revolution. Elections were held in the town of Fort Griffin, or "The Flat" as it was called—a collection of shacks and picket shanties on the flood plain at the foot of the bluff on which the fort was built. Voters installed W. H. Ledbetter as county judge and Henry C. Jacobs as sheriff.

Ledbetter was the first permanent settler of the county. He arrived from his native Georgia and then settled on the Clear Fork in 1859. Forty years old in 1874, he ranched and operated the Ledbetter Salt Works, a Shackelford County landmark. Henry Jacobs, a slim six-footer, was a native of Gallatin County, Kentucky. Neither brought any particular education or experience to his new responsibility, but each was elected because he was considered a man of courage and integrity.[6]

The town of Fort Griffin was the temporary seat of Shackelford County government, but at a special election held there on November 8, 1874, voters made Albany, a village about fourteen miles south of The Flat and more centrally located in the new county, the permanent seat. Removal of the trappings of county government did nothing to temper the boom times in The Flat and may even have contributed to the town's rapidly growing notoriety for lawlessness.

The villages that sprang up near the frontier Texas forts after the Civil War were infamous outlaw haunts. These remote hamlets were ideal locations for horse thieves, cattle rustlers, and stagecoach robbers, who preferred operating on the fringes of populated areas so they could more easily acquire provisions and engage in debauchery. Forts Richardson, Concho, McKavett, Stockton, Davis, and Griffin were all notorious hangouts of outlaw gangs during the seventies. Few records remain of the outlaws who frequented The Flat or of efforts to control them in the years prior to county organization. The recollections of a few area pioneers, however, indicate that in the earliest days the outlaws were opposed by a vigilance committee of seven members who were never identified. This original Shackelford County vigilance organization called itself the Old Law Mob, or simply "OLM."[7]

Collins Creek, a tributary that flows into the Clear Fork of the Brazos near Fort Griffin, was named for one of those who fell victim to the OLM. With no evidence beyond an anonymous accusation that he had unlawfully appropriated some government mules, the vigilantes shot Collins to death by the river and pinned "OLM" on his remains.[8]

Maxwell Creek was also named for a man who figured in the sketchy history of the Old Law Mob. As the story goes, settler

Maxwell and his wife had marital difficulties and there were rumors that the lady had attempted to dispose of her mate by foul means. She then hired a lawyer and sought a divorce, a radical recourse for a woman in that time and place. A party of men called on the attorney and warned him to drop the case. He refused and was ordered to leave the area. Again he refused and soon thereafter was found hanging from the limb of a tree, the tag of the OLM affixed to his coat. The lawyer's body was never buried, but someone cut it down after a few days and threw it into a river ravine.[9]

Collins and the unfortunate lawyer were not outlaws, which made them atypical targets of the OLM. They are probably remembered for that very reason. The horse and cattle thieves who fell victim to vigilantes in the days before the county was organized in 1874 are long forgotten.

Gangs of horse thieves and cattle rustlers ran rampant throughout the frontier counties of northern Texas during the late 1860s and early '70s. Outnumbered and outgunned, county sheriffs—charged with law enforcement responsibility over huge land tracts—were simply incapable of controlling the criminals. During this period of inadequate law enforcement, vigilance organizations were formed in several frontier counties of Texas, but it was in Shackelford County that the night riders were most active because it was at Fort Griffin that the outlaws congregated.

"From 1869 through 1872, cattle stealing in Shackelford County was almost beyond the endurance of both small and large cattle owners," writes a historian of the period. "Everyone was losing cattle. It seemed also as if the outlaws were organized to combat the law organizations. There are instances in which the outlaw groups took letters from the post office and tacked them up for all to read in the local saloons."[10]

A group of Shackelford County settlers identifying themselves only as "Citizens for law and order," dispatched a letter to the Texas governor, pleading for assistance:

We are seriously in need of help. It seems that the local soldiers at the post consider our plight a civilian struggle and will give us no relief. Unless something is done quickly to stop cattle stealing in this part of the country, this area may soon be in civil war.

The cattle thieves are well organized and would dare to fight if challenged. There is no rancher who has not lost cattle.

We are sending this letter to Breckenridge as we are afraid to post it here at Griffin, for it will never get into your hands unless we send it to Breckenridge. By coming to our assistance, you will no doubt prevent bloodshed.[11]

Citizens' complaints like this contributed to quick approval of the county organization petitions and the formation of the Frontier Battalion of the Texas Rangers in 1874. With the establishment of a local law enforcement and judicial system and the hope that the outlaw problem could be handled by legally constituted authorities, the Old Law Mob disbanded. There is no evidence that John Larn was a member of this early organization, although it is clear he was a leader of a later vigilante group.

After a particularly vicious murder in a Fort Griffin saloon in 1872, Maj. W. H. Wood, commanding the garrison at the fort, declared that the land stretching from the bluff to the Clear Fork was part of the government reservation and therefore under his authority. He ordered the immediate evacuation of the saloonmen, gamblers, and prostitutes who had congregated in The Flat. Some of the sporting crowd departed for new pastures, but a few moved no farther than across the Clear Fork, just beyond the army's jurisdiction.[12]

For two years Fort Griffin was relatively tranquil, but after county organization in 1874, the army relinquished control to civilian authorities. Then it was, as one old-timer attested, that the saloons, gambling halls, dance halls, low dives, and every form of vice and lawlessness invaded Fort Griffin and looked to me like all of the bad characters from everywhere were swarming around there. It got so tough there that I was afraid to ride down the streets. . . . It looked like the civil authorities were either helpless or controlled by the lawless element. . . . During those days killings were frequent and I helped bury a number of cowboys killed in shooting scrapes.[13]

Cattle brands were first recorded in Shackelford County on October 1, 1874. On that date John Larn registered two brands, his own HAH and another, exactly the same except the crossbar on the "A" was missing. This second brand was registered in the name of his infant son. One Larn researcher found it "rather charming that a frontier cowman would think of registering a brand for a babe in arms,"[14] but, given his history of brand tampering, Larn may have found it useful to be able to quickly change his son's brand to his own.

The surrender of warring American Indian tribes to U.S. military forces early in 1875 ended the fighting and opened up the Texas plains to the commercial buffalo hunters. They soon made the little shantytown in the shadow of Fort Griffin their headquarters. Even before the Red River War was officially over, hide dealers were organizing and outfitting hunting expeditions at The Flat. On Christmas Day of 1874, Joe McCombs, only twenty years old, led a hunting party out of Fort Griffin that included two future lawmen of note, John W. Poe and John C. Jacobs. Soon the hunters, hide buyers, and outfitting merchandisers poured into Fort Griffin. They were followed by the saloonmen, gamblers and harlots who flocked to every frontier boom town, and The Flat was on its way to becoming the roughest, toughest, wildest camp in Texas.[15]

CHAPTER FIVE

1875: Fort Griffin Debauchery and Larn Domesticity

*"Fort Griffin, when I arrived there, was the toughest place I had
ever seen."*

HENRY HERRON

To Emmett Roberts, the cowman who had the run-in
back in '73 with John Larn, the town of Fort Griffin was "a veritable robber's hole." His experience in The Flat was limited, he said,
because he "tried to keep away from there as much as possible on
account of the lawless conditions at the place. It was dangerous to
put the head out of the window, even while the soldiers were there.
And the soldiers did not break up the lawlessness. They were there
solely to prevent Indian raids. There were not many laws, but even
these were not enforced rigidly."[1]

Twenty-year-old Henry Herron arrived at Fort Griffin from Wisconsin in the summer of 1875. He later recalled his first impression of The Flat: "Fort Griffin, when I arrived there, was the
toughest place I had ever seen. . . . I believe there were eight or ten
saloons there then, and in addition there were several dance halls.

The Bee Hive saloon and dance hall was the main one. Lewd women infested these places, and all of them had their little huts or shanties, which sprawled along the bank of the Clear Fork of the Brazos River. . . ."[2]

Among the sporting crowd—the gamblers, con artists, saloon men, prostitutes, and pimps—that descended on Fort Griffin in 1875 was John Henry "Doc" Holliday, the tubercular dentist turned gambler, and his lover, "Big Nose" Kate Elder. Holliday would later gain frontier immortality as the sixshooter sidekick of Wyatt Earp in Kansas and Arizona. Others, forgotten today, but well known in the frontier boom camps of the time, included Mike Lynch, Bill Reed, Bill Henderson, James Oglesby, Frank Smith, Tom Grise, Isaac Blum, Owen Donnelly, Patrick Carroll, and "Hurricane Bill" Martin. With them came their female counterparts, Lottie Deno, "Long Kate," Mollie McCabe, Maggie Marshall, and Jessie Tye, a.k.a. "Hurricane Minnie," the consort of Hurricane Bill.[3]

In a response to the new arrivals, the Shackelford County grand jury met for the first time in January 1875. Indictments were handed down against William A. Hurricane Bill Martin, Doc Holliday, and a bevy of females identified only as "Liz," "Etta," "Kate," and so forth, on charges ranging from "gaming in a saloon" to "keeping a disorderly house."[4] The new officials were putting into effect a practice long found useful in frontier towns, the raising of governmental revenue off the wages of sin. Gambling was ubiquitous, prostitution was open and pervasive, and the authorities, recognizing the value these attractions could have for a booming frontier economy, had no desire to stamp them out. Convictions and the resulting fines were intended only to generate funds for the operation of county government.

Fort Griffin was the center of county government for only a short time, so an official courthouse was never established there. The county commissioners' minutes for July 1875 show payments of $15 to W. L. Browning for use of his residence as a district court, and $10 to H. C. Smith for use of his house as a grand jury room.

Fort Griffin in the 1870s, considered by many frontier veterans to be the toughest town in Texas.

At this same time the commissioners authorized construction of a permanent courthouse at Albany. It was to be 45 by 20 feet in size, built of pickets, and roofed with cypress shingles.[5] There seems to have been no established municipal authority at Fort Griffin, but businessmen later appointed and paid for a badly needed town marshal.

The response to violence in The Flat was often more violence. In October 1875 Sheriff Jacobs killed a man at Fort Griffin in the line of duty. Just before daybreak on September 12, four men had stormed the building serving as a jail at Jacksboro in neighboring Jack County, overpowered the guards, and released all the prisoners.[6] On October 12 Sheriff Jacobs spotted one of the escapees, a black man named George Conn, also known as William Corn, in the Flat. When the sheriff attempted arrest, Conn fled. After calling on him to halt, Jacobs fired, killing the fugitive.[7]

Although it is likely that many shootings and stabbings went unrecorded, a particularly cowardly and brutal murder in December 1875 received statewide attention. At dusk on the evening of December 22 Andy Brownlee was seated at a gambling table near a window of the Bee Hive saloon. A rough character on horseback, named James P. Oglesby, approached the window. Drawing a pistol and taking careful aim at Brownlee's head, he fired, put spurs to his horse, and thundered out of town. Brownlee died within minutes. Sheriff Jacobs rounded up a posse of ten men and rode in pursuit, but lost the trail in the dark. Oglesby was one of what a newspaper called "a strong gang of about thirty desperadoes [who] rule the country surrounding Griffin."[8]

The Shackelford County grand jury brought an indictment for murder against Oglesby the following May, but he was still named on the Texas sheriffs' list of wanted fugitives two years later.[9]

John Larn, who did not drink, smoke, gamble, or consort with lewd women, was involved in none of this Fort Griffin tumult. He was busy building a new home for his family across the Clear Fork from the Honeymoon Cottage. Still inhabited after more than a

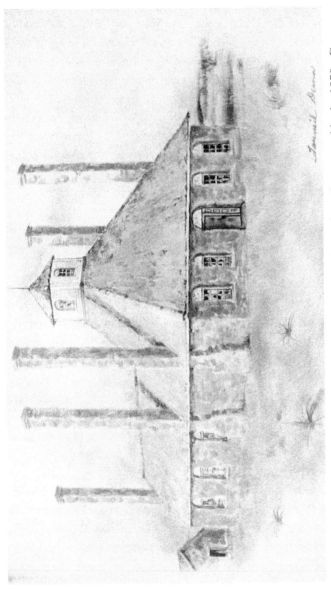

An artist's conception of the Larn ranch house, complete with cupola, as it appeared in the 1870s. Courtesy of Julia Putnam.

century and a quarter, the remarkable dwelling that Larn designed and constructed, even after several renovations, stands as a silent testimony to the man's talents. Far ahead of its time for frontier Texas, the L-shaped, single-story house was constructed of thick stone at a time when picket houses were the norm. It had six large rooms and a spacious attic. From five mantled fireplaces, tall chimneys rose beyond the peak of the roof, upon which was built a square, glassed-in cupola. According to local legend, this cupola was intended to serve as Larn's watchtower. The dining room occupied a wing extending from the main body of the house. It had a high ceiling ornamented by one of the house's most distinguishing features, a beautiful octagonal medallion that Larn designed and constructed by fitting together more than two hundred separate moldings around a central pendant. A kerosene lamp was suspended from the center of the medallion in Larn's time, before the house was electrified. Other refinements included handsome wooden mantles above the fireplaces, elaborate paneling at the windows, curved arches above interior doorways, and narrow lights of etched glass on both sides of the main door. Around a well and cistern situated in the ell of the building, Larn built a porch. Outbuildings included a large stone smokehouse, a barn, and a springhouse near the river.[10]

On March 24, 1875, a second son was born to John and Mary Larn and christened Joseph Beck after his maternal grandfather. Sadly, this child lived only six months and died on September 17. The Larns buried the infant near the new house.

In May Larn had his 160-acre homestead surveyed by George A. Kirkland.[11] Even as he worked his growing cattle herds, the ever-energetic and ambitious young rancher managed a freighting business, hauling buffalo hides and meat from Fort Griffin to Fort Worth. The ever-present John Selman partnered him in the enterprise.

On May 31 Larn and Selman, as well as several drivers and freight handlers in their employ, were camped on the banks of the

The first child of John and Mary Jane Larn survived only six months and was buried near the ranch house. Courtesy of Julia Putnam.

Brazos waiting for the spring floodwaters to recede so they could cross. They had four wagons, each drawn by six yoke of oxen. The animals had been turned out to graze while the men waited. In the late afternoon the skies darkened, and an ominous wedge-shaped cloud appeared in the west and moved toward them. The men ran for the wagons and barely reached them before the tornado struck. Buffalo hides were ripped from the wagons and scattered over the countryside. One wagon was completely destroyed and the other three were badly damaged. Two drivers were lifted thirty feet into the air and dropped some distance from camp but, miraculously, did not suffer serious injury. After the storm passed, Larn found a large four-year-old steer deposited nearby that the tornado had apparently transported many miles. Larn and Selman had to go back to Fort Griffin for new wagons. When they returned to the site they had to spend several days searching for their scattered buffalo hides, many of which were never recovered.[12] The Larn-Selman freighting venture ended soon after this disastrous tornado incident, and Larn refocused his energy on the business of cattle.

Horse and cattle thievery was again on the increase in the Clear Fork country in 1875, as documented by the Texas press. Shackelford County had no paper of its own at this time, but newspapers around the state were kept informed of local events by frequent letters from Shackelford residents.

"Quite a number of horse and cattle thieves have made their appearance in this neighborhood," one correspondent reported in February. "There are daily complaints made to the Post Commander about these outrages."[13]

The coming national centennial year of 1876 would see John Larn emerge as a central figure in the ongoing war between stockmen and rustlers, and this time he would be wearing a badge.

CHAPTER SIX

1876: Sheriff Larn and the Tin Hat-Band Brigade

"Where bad men band together for the purpose of committing robbery, . . . it seems as though no medicine will reach the case but blue whistlers or hemp."

JACKSBORO FRONTIER ECHO
April 28, 1876

The spring of 1876 brought two important developments to Shackelford County and the Clear Fork country: the election of John Larn as sheriff and the emergence of a new vigilante organization. The two events were not unrelated. The vigilantes, calling themselves the "Tin Hat-Band Brigade," or simply "Tin Hats,"[1] would remain active for more than two years. Their activities would focus attention on Fort Griffin and Shackelford County from throughout Texas and across the nation. John Larn, as sheriff, would lead the vigilantes in many of their actions, but in time he himself would become the chief target of the mob organization and be destroyed by it.

The defeat of the Comanche, Kiowa, and Arapaho tribes by the

U.S. Army in the Red River campaign of 1874–75 virtually brought an end to Indian raids on the stock of northern Texas settlers. However, a different element soon replaced the Native marauders from Indian Territory. Gangs of white thieves began preying on the ranchers, stealing horses and cattle and driving the stock across the Red River to sell at the Indian agencies or Kansas markets. By early 1876 the rowdy town below Fort Griffin had become the headquarters for these outlaw gangs.

Formation of the Tin Hat-Band Brigade and the election of Larn as county sheriff were direct responses to the influx of outlaws. Although the total number of vigilante members and their identities have never been made public, and, even over a century later, participation by certain individuals remains a matter of local dispute, there is no doubt the membership was extensive and included most of the leading citizens of the region. Sgt. J. E. Van Riper of the Texas Rangers, stationed near Fort Griffin in 1878, estimated the organization's membership as "upwards of one hundred and fifty persons."[2]

John Larn's leadership in the Tin Hat committee has never been questioned. Interviews with local residents thirty years later convinced researcher Don L. Biggers that Larn had been "a long time chief in the vigilance committee."[3] Frank Collinson, who hunted buffalo in the region during these years and frequently visited Fort Griffin, said the Tin Hat organization "was composed of businessmen, cowmen, horse ranchmen, county officers, and a few buffalo hunters. Both Lorn and Selman were members."[4]

A list of Shackelford County vigilantes, discovered in the files of the Texas Adjutant General by the late Dr. C. L. Sonnichsen in 1944, included many prominent citizens and officers of the law: W. H. Ledbetter, county judge; Cornelius K. Stribling, lawyer, land agent, and the minister of the gospel who had united John and Mary Larn in marriage; Henry Jacobs, the county's first sheriff; John Jacobs, Henry's brother and a later sheriff; William R. Cruger, another sheriff; W. C. Gilson, the city marshal at Fort Griffin; James

Draper, a deputy sheriff; G. Riley Carter, the constable who participated with Larn in the Bush Knob massacre; John W. Poe, deputy sheriff and city marshal at Fort Griffin; and well-known cattlemen John Jackson, George Mathews, and Samuel Conner. Sonnichsen speculated that the list had been provided to the Texas Rangers by John Selman. He doubted its thrustworthiness and thought it was not "a good thing to have lying around."[5]

In a letter to Maj. John B. Jones, commander of the Frontier Battalion of the Texas Rangers, Sergeant Van Riper reported that Edgar Rye, justice of the peace and county coroner, was "known to be a member of a certain Clan in this county," i.e. the Tin Hat-Band Brigade.[6] In his 1909 book, *The Quirt and the Spur,* Rye never admitted to membership in the organization but made it clear he approved of its activities. The Tin Hat-Band Brigade, he said, was composed of "the brave men of the frontier of Texas who, in the absence of protection under the law, were forced to band themselves together for the mutual protection of their lives and property." He said he "did not remember a single instance of the wrongful use of the power of the Vigilance Committee that operated around Fort Griffin."[7]

Shackelford County voters on February 15, 1876, elected John Larn sheriff. Two weeks short of his twenty-seventh birthday, he became the chief law enforcement officer of not only Shackelford, but also a vast expanse of territory. The many unorganized counties under Larn's control—from Stephens to the east, Throckmorton to the north, Callahan to the south, and a dozen others extending all the way to the New Mexico Territory line—had been attached to Shackelford for administrative purposes.[8]

Larn did not officially take office until April 18, after he had made bond.[9] It was during this two-month period between Larn's election and assumption of office that the Tin Hats first went into action.

As Shackelford County did not have a newspaper until January 1879, published accounts from before 1879 are available only

Edgar Rye, justice of the peace and coroner, later wrote a book recounting historic events of Shackleford County. Courtesy of Charles M. Robinson III.

through local correspondents who regularly reported on Clear Fork events to newspapers around the state: "Sigma" of the *Galveston Daily News*, "Lone Star" of the *Fort Worth Daily Democrat*, and the *Fort Worth Weekly Democrat*, "Comanche Jim" of the *Dallas Daily Herald*, Carl Schulz of the *San Antonio Daily Herald*, and "Clear Fork" of the *Jacksboro Frontier Echo*.[10]

One of the earliest reports of renewed vigilante activity came from Lone Star. Near The Flat one night early in April,[11] Charles McBride and Calvin Sharp, two notorious horse thieves, attempted to drive off some horses belonging to local Tonkawa and Lipan tribesmen. Several Indians and white men went in pursuit, engaged the outlaws in a running gunfight, and forced them to abandon the stolen horses and flee. Later Sharp, critically injured, returned to town and was apprehended. His captors took him to the fort hospital where the post surgeon pronounced the wounds fatal. On the morning of April 11 Charles McBride was found "lariated to a tree" on the banks of the Clear Fork. "By inadvertence, perhaps, one end of the rope encircled his neck," reported Lone Star.[12]

Comanche Jim wrote that McBride had been "caught in the very act of taking what wasn't his'n" and vigilantes had suspended him from a pecan tree. They left a pick and shovel under the corpse for the convenience of anyone who might want to bury the dead man,[13] and pinned a note to the body: "He said his name was McBride, but he was a liar as well as a thief."[14] Comanche Jim commented, "So far, so good. As long as the committee strings up the right parties, it has the well wishes of every lover of tranquility."[15]

John Larn apparently was not involved in the McBride lynching, as he and other members of the Tin Hat-Band Brigade were busy chasing other horse thieves at the time. On April 2 near the Mackenzie crossing of the Clear Fork, an outlaw gang led by Wellington "Bill" Henderson made off with twenty-six horses belonging to the Ellison, Dewees, and Bishop cattle-driving outfit.[16] Riding with Henderson were a Jacksboro desperado named Joe

Watson, "Larapie Dan" Moran, Dan "Red" McClusky, Henry "Hank" Floyd, and one identified only as "Kansas Bill."

Sheriff-elect Larn and a party of vigilantes that included his brother-in-law and newly elected county assessor John A. Matthews set out from Fort Griffin in pursuit on April 3. They were accompanied by a mounted military unit under the command of 2nd Lt. William W. Shipman of the 11th U.S. Infantry. The detail consisted of a corporal, a private, and Government Scout Henry W. Strong in charge of ten Tonkawa Indian trackers.[17] The outcome of this expedition had eerie overtones of the Bush Knob Massacre back in 1873 when Larn rode at the head of a similar civilian and military posse.

A few miles above the Clear Fork the outlaw gang had split. Henderson, Hank Floyd, and Kansas Bill hurried northward with the majority of the stolen horses, while the rest of the gang followed with a heavy wagon and team. In the slower party were Watson, Moran, McClusky, and two others, a buffalo hunter named Burr and a veteran frontier boom-camp hooker known as Mrs. Wolf. She began calling herself Sally Watson after establishing an attachment to Joe Watson.

After following the trail for eighty miles, the Larn posse overtook Watson and company on Croton Creek in western Haskell County.[18] Henry Strong has left a succinct account of what then transpired: "Just at daylight . . . we rode up to them in camp. Mrs. Wolf and Joe Watson were in the gang. When we dismounted [the lieutenant] ordered them to surrender and they began firing. They were all shot down, save Mrs. Wolf."[19] According to contemporary newspaper accounts, Watson, Larapie Dan, and Red McClusky were wounded in the gunfight, captured, strung up, and dispatched on a journey "to a land where horses will not be required." There was said to be "much rejoicing among the good citizens of Griffin . . . over the affair as the men were notorious desperadoes and the country is better off" without them.[20] Lone Star found the news of Watson's passing particularly welcome: "Watson was a noted

Army Scout Henry Strong accompanied a Larn posse in pursuit of horse thieves.

desperado here and at Jacksboro, and this community feels relieved at the assurance that his pistol shots and yells will no longer be heard in our streets."[21]

The posse led by Sheriff-elect Larn and Lieutenant Shipman[22] arrived back at Fort Griffin on April 10 with Burr and Sally Watson as prisoners. Although one newspaper report characterized Burr as "a notorious horse-thief," the authorities released him after interrogation, indicating that in this affair, at least, he was an innocent bystander. They also released Sally Watson to return to her former haunts in the vice resorts of The Flat. Notices were dispatched to law enforcement officers at points north to be on the lookout for Bill Henderson and the rest of his gang who were headed that way with their stolen horses.

On April 18 Larn took his oath of office as sheriff of Shackelford County and immediately appointed as deputy his crony, Old John Selman.[23] Two nights later the vigilante nightriders struck again.

The previous week City Marshal William C. "Big Bill" Gilson had surprised one Houston Faught, described by the *Jacksboro Frontier Echo* as "a well-known desperate character," in the act of stealing a horse. In making the arrest Gilson put a bullet in Faught and then delivered him wounded to the hospital at the fort where he was held under guard. At eleven o'clock on the night of April 20, "a party of mounted men, armed and disguised," overpowered the guard and took charge of the prisoner. They hauled him out to the Clear Fork and hanged him from a tree. A card pinned to his clothing identified him as "Horse Thief No. 5," indicating that he followed McBride, Watson, Moran, and McClusky on the Tin Hat committee's death list. The card also charged Faught with murdering a boy and scalping the body to shift the blame to Indians. It asked, "Shall horse thieves rule the country?" and added an ominous threat: "He will have company soon."[24]

Editor G. W. Robson of the *Jacksboro Frontier Echo* had denounced vigilantism only two months before. "It seems at times instead of progression we have retrogression in a violent form," he wrote in the issue of February 11. The citizenry, "not content with the slow but sure workings of the law, [resort to] lynch law. . . . Northern journals comment in severe terms upon us as a community of murderers and robbers, and can we with truth deny the accusation?"

But by April, Robson seemed to approve of the Tin Hat campaign. The hanging of Faught, he said,

> ends the career of a man who has led a life of crime and created trouble and sorrow wherever he sojourned. A few more of the same sort are left, but they will give Shackelford county a wide berth if they know when they are well off. . . .
>
> We do not believe in mob law or violence in any form, but where bad men band together for the purpose of committing robbery, and the members of such law breaking organizations are possessed of influence enough to enable its members to escape the penalty of the law, as is believed to be the case in Shackelford county, it seems as though no medicine will reach the case but blue whistlers or hemp. . . . The stealing of horses has become so frequent that the losers could not purchase fresh stock fast enough to satisfy the demand of the horse thief. The people have arisen in their might and declared that thieves shall no longer rule the country.[25]

Faught had barely been disposed of when Larn received word from Ford County Sheriff Charles E. Bassett at Dodge City, Kansas, that he had nabbed Bill Henderson on April 24 and was holding him.[26] Larn hurried to Dodge City, where he also took into custody Henry Floyd, "another joker of the same stripe."[27] Larn had to wait for extradition papers to be forwarded from Austin and did not arrive back in Fort Griffin with his prisoners until June 1.[28]

He found that the Tin Hats had not been idle during his absence. On May 2 they had captured a "notorious character known as 'Reddy' of horse theft fame" and ensconced him in the Fort Griffin guardhouse. Three days later officers arrived to take him to Eastland County, where he was wanted on horse theft charges. On May 6 his body was found hanging from a tree three miles from Fort Griffin. "One by One the Roses Fall; Court Proceedings on the Clear Fork, Judge Lynch Presiding" ran the headline in the *Jacksboro Frontier Echo.*[29]

Now thoroughly incited, the vigilantes did not limit their attention to stock thieves. Looking to The Flat where outlaws congregated, they issued warnings to those who attracted the undesirable element. They posted a notice announcing that the presence of "Long Kate"; "Big Billy"; prostitutes Ellen Gentry, Minnie Gray, and Sally Watson; and "general rustlers" "Pony" Spencer and Tom Riley would no longer be tolerated in Fort Griffin, and those named were warned to leave by a specified hour. The notice was embellished by "a hideous caricature of a death's head and crossbones in sanguinary colors." [30] Soon Fort Griffin correspondent Comanche Jim reported that the vigilantes, "motivated by the idea that bad meat draws flies in the persons of horse thieves and desperadoes," had broken up "a nest of prostitutes and the soiled birds had flown."[31]

When some of the "soiled birds" flew back a couple of months later, the *Jacksboro Frontier Echo* reported that a new placard had been posted between the telegraph office and Owen Donnelly's saloon:

Notice! Notice!
More Trouble! More Trouble!
We've given notice that no prostitutes will be suffered to come among us. Several have come in the last few days. We know the parties who persuaded them to come. When we strike, look out. We wait a little. The prostitutes are less to blame than the men who bring them and keep them, but all will suffer. Leave or you are doomed.

—Vigilance.[32]

Sheriff Larn, after returning from Kansas with Henderson and Floyd, first lodged his prisoners in the guardhouse at Fort Griffin, since Shackelford County had no jail at the time. Then, on June 3, he transferred them to a room in the county courthouse, still under construction, at Albany. They did not remain there long. That night the guards, nineteen-year-old George Wilhelm and another young fellow named Berner, were confronted and disarmed, they said, "by a large body of about fifty men afoot and twenty mounted."[33]

Sigma, in his letter to the *Galveston Daily News,* made sport of this account, saying the guards were overwhelmed by "about fifty men, something less than seventeen feet tall, with guns about four inches across at the muzzle."[34] There were only six or eight in the Tin Hat party, according to another report.[35]

The vigilantes seized the prisoners and the guards and marched them all to a grove of trees on Hubbard Creek, a quarter mile out of town. It was said that as ropes were being prepared, Henderson cried like a child but Floyd remained calm, stoically accepting his fate. After stringing up the two men, the Tin Hats set Wilhelm and Berner free and silently departed. The morning light found Floyd hanging low in the tree, his feet nearly touching the ground. Henderson was suspended in the same tree, much farther up. "The vigilantes mean business," concluded a special telegram that provided the gruesome details to the *Galveston Daily News.*[36]

A coroner's jury found that Henderson and Floyd came to their deaths by strangulation at the hands of parties unknown. The bodies were buried in a potter's field and that was the end of that. In a June 3 letter to the *Jacksboro Frontier Echo,* Clear Fork admitted that it was "a deplorable state of affairs when Judge Lynch is called to preside," but pointed out that the "vigilantes, tall, tin-hat fellows, [had] made no mistakes. There is nothing like knowing your man."[37]

This lynching received statewide coverage in the press, but some of the facts were garbled. Several newspaper accounts named Sheriff Larn as one of the guards overpowered by the mob.[38] Since Larn was a leader of the Tin Hat-Band Brigade, it is unlikely there would have been a raid on the prisoners while he was at the jail. It is more probable that Larn, masked, was himself one of the lynch mob. There was little hint of opprobrium in news accounts of the work of the Tin Hat committee. The *Austin Weekly Statesman,* for instance, merely mentioned that Henderson and Floyd, "horse thieves and scoundrels," were hanged at Albany in Shackelford County.[39]

In less than two months the Shackelford County vigilantes had disposed of eight accused outlaws. There may have been others during this spate of Tin Hat activity that went unreported. Edgar Rye, who, as county coroner, had reason to know, later wrote that the mob hanged outlaws Jim Townsend and Andy Brownlee at the same time they disposed of McBride.[40] Seth Hathaway, who hunted buffalo near Fort Griffin during this period, recalled that Tom Cox, another hide hunter and a deserter from the U.S. Army, joined the Bill Henderson gang of horse thieves and was hanged by the vigilantes at the same time as Henderson and Floyd.[41]

Public opinion in the Clear Fork country unquestionably supported the Tin Hat campaign. Editor Robson over in Jacksboro reflected the general sentiment when he scoffed at a suggestion in the *McKinney Enquirer* that legislation be enacted making the punishment for first, second, and third horse theft convictions whipping, branding, and hanging, in that order. "Get out with your nonsense," sneered Robson. "What's the use of all that bother? Hang 'em first; then if they persist in their amusement, cremate them. If that does not put the kibosh on 'em, we don't know what will."[42]

Two years later Robson quoted estimates that horse thefts in Texas totaled 100,000 over the previous three years. Although it was believed as many as 750 criminals were engaged in the business, not more than one in ten had been captured and brought to justice. "By common practice in rural districts," he said,

> every man caught is either shot on the spot or hung on the nearest tree. And no instance is yet recorded where the law paid the slightest attention to lynchers of this kind. It is

conceded by judge and jury that the man who steals a horse in Texas forfeits his life to the owner. It is a game of life and death. Men will pursue these thieves for 500 miles, go to any length, spend any amount of money, and fight them to the death when overtaken. That they will be exterminated admits of no doubt. The poor scoundrels cannot last long when the feeling of our civilization is so aroused against them as it now is in Texas.[43]

As a Shackelford County historian has pointed out, the theft of a horse during this period caused more excitement than a murder. Federal troops joined civilians to pursue stock thieves—the Bush Knob and Watson affairs were two examples—but never to catch murderers. Although civil law officers arrested some murder suspects in Fort Griffin, few were tried and *none* were convicted.[44]

The Tin Hat-Band Brigade made the same distinction, according to Phin Reynolds: "All of the men killed by the Vigilance Committee, to the best of my information, were killed for stealing. None of them were killed for having murdered any one."[45]

In a letter to the editors of the *Galveston Daily News* from Fort Griffin on June 6, 1876, Sigma said:

You have no doubt heard many reports of men being found hung or shot in this part of the State, which are calculated to convey a wrong impression of the actual state of affairs existing on this portion of the border. In many instances the rumors circulated, and which not infrequently find their way into type, are without foundation, and serve to deter immigrants from locating on the frontier.

Within the past two months five or six men have been found hanging from the trees in this vicinity. No one seems to know how they got there, nor are they sufficiently interested in the matter to inquire, though the public verdict is suicide under the influence of remorse, caused by the larceny of a horse. The learned Esculapius of this place says: "Death ensued from congestion of the brain, occasioned by compression of the carotid artery, produced by the contraction of a rope." If the above verdicts are correct, in either case no one but the victim is to blame, as it is plain the aforesaid contraction was caused by his own weight. It is well known that in every instant there is sufficient proof to establish the character of the victims as horse thieves beyond question.

The effect of these hangings has been to make Griffin one of the most orderly towns in the State. The citizens feel secure in the possession of property, while thieves and vagrants seem to regard the town as an unattractive place of resort.[46]

For some months following the lively vigilante activity in the spring of 1876, Clear Fork settlers experienced a period of relative calm. Horse thievery and cattle rustling greatly diminished as outlaws departed for more propitious haunts. Sheriff Larn was credited for the improvement, although much of it had been accomplished by extralegal means. Even Edgar Rye, certainly no admirer of Larn, whom he accused of "cunning thievery and redhanded murder,"[47] had to admit that Larn as sheriff "did more to quell lawlessness than any man . . . before or since his time."[48]

However, not everyone agreed with the view that acquiescence by law enforcement officials to vigilante demands and open participation in their activities was beneficial or necessary even on a rough frontier. In May 1876, Editor Robson of the *Jacksboro Frontier Echo* reminded his readers of Governor Richard Coke's remarks on law enforcement during his inaugural address the previous January.

> It should be made a rule of evidence, a legal presumption, when a jail is forced and prisoners taken out and murdered or are rescued by their friends, that the sheriff and jailer are accessories to the crime, devolving upon them, if innocent, the

burden of proving their innocence. A *bona fide* defense against such attacks would always attract such attention as to be susceptible of proof. . . .

No sheriff should be permitted to hold office another day after his jail has been forced, unless he can prove an actual *bona fide* determined resistance. . . . I have never heard of a sheriff or a jailer being hurt, or of one of them hurting any of the assailants. Nor have I ever known a *bona fide* resolute resistance made by a sheriff or a jailer to the demands of a mob fail to be successful.[49]

J. R. Fleming, judge of the district court, echoed the governor's comments in his charge to the Shackelford County grand jury in June. It was, he said, a "shame and disgrace" that the citizenry had become impatient with the court system and had "thrown off and trampled under foot the wholesome restraint of the law," attempting "the uncertain, precarious and very dangerous" practice of self-administration of justice. Vigilantes excused their crimes on the grounds that the courts had failed and that their vigilantism was justified by the basic law of self-preservation. "The courts, the juries, and the county officials, gentlemen, are responsible for these infractions of the law," said Fleming.

The whole moral guilt, disguise it as we may, lies at the door of these public functionaries, and upon them as well as the community at large should the odium rest. . . . There's nothing that contributes so much to the maintenance of peace and good order in your country, nothing that tends so much to the repression of crime, as the prompt, efficient and impartial discharge of the duties devolving on county officials; on the other hand, there is nothing that encourages bold bad men so much to violate the law and trample under their feet the authorities charged with enforcement as the loose and careless habits of county officials.[50]

Despite the disapproval of governor and judge, popular opinion in Shackelford County favored the actions of the Tin Hat-Band Brigade. "The vigilantes seem to be doing good work in ridding the country of thieves and desperadoes," wrote Lone Star in the pages of the *Fort Worth Weekly Democrat.* "This is severe remedy, but desperate cases require desperate remedies, and we must think the Fort Griffin people justifiable in protecting their lives and property."[51]

The editors of the *Galveston Daily News* thought the vigilante activity in Shackelford County was "to be regretted," but recognized "in mitigation of the summary proceedings" that the county had become "so thickly settled with horse thieves and cut-throats that it was impossible for law-abiding citizens to keep a horse in their possession."[52]

Looking back on the period from a perspective of nearly seventy years, Phin Reynolds was certain the work of the Tin Hats was appropriate and necessary. "The hangings and killings of the ones accused of stealing had a good effect in stopping thievery in this country," he told researcher J. R. Webb in 1945. "After this time, there was less stealing here than anywhere I know of."[53]

The Tin Hat membership included most of the leading men of the county. Therefore, participation by John Larn and John Selman, stockmen of substance, was not considered unusual, even though the two happened to be the county sheriff and his chief deputy.

The summer of 1876 passed with no more reports of night riding by the Tin Hat-Band Brigade. Tensions eased and Shackelford County citizens concentrated on business activity. Commerce in buffalo hides was at its peak. A Clear Fork old-timer recalled that in 1876, merchant Frank E. Conrad "had buffalo hides stacked higher than a man's head and covering about ten acres of ground."[54] John C. Irwin recalled seeing hides at Fort Griffin "stacked tier upon tier, in rows," making the place look like a great lumberyard.[55] In April, Lone Star enthused in his Fort Worth correspondence: "Buffalo hides are coming in in large numbers, and the trade will doubtless be kept up well into the summer, if, indeed, there be any cessation whatever."[56] A week later he reported that "buffalo hides from the west and cattle from the south are coming in rapidly. . . . Griffin is now about the only market for buffalo hides, and as the bovines are being rapidly decimated it will probably be the last market."[57]

As noted by Lone Star, more and more south Texas ranchers, driving their herds to the northern markets, had deserted the old Chisholm Trail to the east for the newly established Western Cattle Trail that passed by Fort Griffin. The drovers, stopping to rest and recreate at Fort Griffin before the final long drive into Dodge City, brought a new infusion of business activity to the little town. "The cattle trail to the north via this point, Cantonment and Dodge City is now an assured fact," said Lone Star, adding that it was estimated 125,000 head would come up the trail that season.[58]

Fort Griffin's prosperity was noted around the state. The *Galveston Daily News* reported in July that the town now had several stores, a hotel, a steam sawmill, a baker, and a shoemaker. Buffalo-hide buyer J. J. Hickey had by that season already purchased fifty thousand dollars' worth of hides and had shipped out over one million pounds of the product.[59]

In 1876 merchants Charles Meyer and E. Frankel built the first permanent business houses in Fort Griffin. Each store contained a saloon that the owner claimed was the finest west of Fort Worth. Meyer's saloon was noteworthy for providing ice for drinks throughout most of the summer months; Frankel chose to use his precious ice to preserve fresh seafood for the enjoyment of his customers.[60]

John C. Irwin thought that the 1876–77 period was unquestionably Fort Griffin's peak of prosperity: "There were buffalo hunters, hide money, trail money, trail herd money, and soldier money, and too, it was the provisioning point for settlers going west and north."[61]

While Fort Griffin boomed, Albany, the county seat and the only other "town" worthy of that designation in Shackelford County,

remained a tiny village. Other than the frame courthouse, the only
structures in Albany in 1876 were one storehouse and three resi-
dences. The little community was situated on a prairie dog town,
and there were many more prairie dogs than people.[62]

In addition to pursuing outlaws, the enterprising and ambitious
John Larn continued to build up his wealth as he actively traded in
cattle and land that eventful year of 1876. In February he sold 103
cows and one yearling to Proctor A. Graham for $1,230, receiving
$400 down with the balance due by April 1. As Larn retained a lien
on the cattle, he and Graham both signed the sales agreement,
which displayed the animals' marks and brands, and recorded it at
the Shackelford County courthouse.[63] The peculiar mixture of
brands and marks on the animals raises the eyebrows of cattlemen
even a century later:

> Only three had H A H, Larn's brand, with no other brand, and
> ten did not have his counter brand. Two of those had – A H
> as a counter brand. Most of the cattle were branded on both
> sides and all but nine had both ears marked. Curiously, the
> counter-branded cows had some 57 brands other than the
> Larn brand on them, a strange collection for a ranchman.[64]

One could easily conclude that Larn was selling off a bunch of
cattle that, as Comanche Jim might say, "wasn't his'n."

Using part of the proceeds of this sale, Larn invested in some
Fort Griffin property a few weeks later, paying John Selman $100
for two town lots.[65]

In August Larn filed for title to the 160 acres of public land he
had homesteaded on the Clear Fork. He swore in his application
that he was a *bona fide* settler, the head of a family, and that for three
consecutive years, beginning July 20, 1873, he had occupied and
improved the property surveyed for him in 1875. Testifying to the
truth of Larn's claim were two of his neighbors, John Selman and
Martin Van Buren Hoover.[66] Shackelford County Clerk J. N.

Masterton took Larn's deposition on August 21, a certificate of occupancy was filed on September 13, and Governor Coke formally granted Larn's patent on October 10.[67]

That same August, Larn entered the business of breeding prize Durham cattle. He paid H. C. Moore $500 for five fine animals— three heifers and two bulls—all less than three years old.[68] But tick-carried Texas fever, a disease to which native longhorns were immune but proved deadly to imported stock, quickly struck Larn's prize Durhams. One of his bulls died a month after the sale. Larn told friends the animal was worth $400.[69]

Larn signed a lease arrangement with J. M. Goff, a prominent rancher of Stonewall County, in November. Goff agreed to range one hundred cows and fifty-two calves of Larn's for a period of five years, after which time the two men would share in the increase.[70] In the light of John Larn's penchant for acquiring cattle with brands other than his own, this appears to have been a scheme to move some stock of questionable origin to a more distant range where the original owners would be less likely to find them.

Despite his duties as sheriff and many business and ranching activities, Larn found time that summer for diversions such as horse racing and politics. One horse race promoted by Pete Haverty, a Fort Griffin livery stable owner and track enthusiast, caused a furor when race officials declared Larn had won an extremely close race by precisely three inches. "Some dissatisfaction was manifested by the decision," reported Lone Star. Bettors were amazed that the judges could be "endowed with vision of such mathematical nicety as to be able to determine the exact number of inches the winning horse was ahead at the string." It is perhaps significant that the judges were Jack Greathouse, who Lone Star characterized as a "bootlegger," and Larn's close friend and associate, John Selman.[71]

A presidential election was held in 1876, and solidly Democratic Shackelford County stood foursquare behind Democrat Samuel Tilden in his race to defeat Republican candidate Rutherford B.

Hayes. On August 9 voters gathered in Fort Griffin to elect delegates to the Democratic Congressional Convention scheduled to be held in Dallas on August 30. They selected Fort Griffin freighter, merchant, and hotelman Henry Clay "Hank" Smith as delegation chairman and J. W. Myers, a former army lieutenant who had been stationed at the fort, as secretary. Representing the various county districts were Judge W. H. Ledbetter, cattleman George O. Mathews, County Clerk J. N. Masterton, lawyer Cornelius K. Stribling, and Sheriff John Larn.[72]

When Larn returned to Fort Griffin after the Congressional Convention, he was back to business as usual. According to a story told by Joe McCombs, a veteran of the early days of Fort Griffin, Larn twice saved the life of a buffalo hunter in October 1876. The man, an unreconstructed Rebel, got drunk in The Flat and decided to go up the bluff and "run all them damn Yankees out." A pistol in each hand, he flushed a bevy of black troopers from the mess hall. When the post commander learned of the disturbance, he sent a lieutenant "to prepare a firing squad, proceed to the mess hall, and kill the intruder." At about the same time, Sheriff Larn got wind of the goings-on and hurried to the fort, arriving before the "firing squad" took action. He requested and received permission to take the drunk into his custody. He led the man out of the mess hall, took him down to The Flat, and deposited him in a vacant shack to sleep off his bender. To make certain the fellow stayed put, Larn braced the door shut with a log.

Awakening later, cold and still inebriated, the man built a fire in the windowless shack. Soon the whole building was aflame. Unable to escape because of the blocked door, the man was near death from burns and smoke inhalation when Larn raced back and dragged him out.[73]

Late in the year horse thieves drifted back into the Clear Fork country and resumed their activities. The Tin Hat-Band Brigade again went to work. In the December 19 issue of the *Fort Worth Daily Democrat*, Lone Star reported that vigilantes trailed eleven outlaws who had stolen twenty-seven horses, overtook them seven miles west of The Flat, and hanged all eleven on the spot. Another Tin Hat party followed four gang members across the Red River and captured them before they reached Fort Sill. At last reports the four were being returned to Fort Griffin, but Lone Star doubted any could expect to live a long life. The *Democrat* commented editorially that "the vigilantes seem to be doing good work in ridding the country of thieves and desperadoes. This is a severe remedy, but desperate cases require severe remedies, and we must think the Fort Griffin people justifiable in protecting their lives and property."[74]

The story seems exaggerated and it is unlikely that the vigilantes lynched eleven or more men at this time, but the extent of their work will never be known. Anecdotal recollections of old-timers provide some details, however.

Hank Smith, proprietor of the Occidental Hotel in Fort Griffin, claimed that boarders greeted him on more than one morning with the offhand comment: "We have another man for breakfast hanging down yonder in a tree."[75]

Frank Collinson recalled that out on the buffalo range "every time we had news from Griffin we learned someone had been hanging from a tree along the Clear Fork." Once when he went to town for supplies, he came upon two men dangling from the limb of a pecan tree. A notice pinned to the clothes of one of the corpses warned: "Anyone moving these men will fill their places." Collinson, no fool, rode on.

He remembered in vivid detail a personal brush with the Tin Hats. He and his partner, Jim White, were approached at their buffalo camp along the Salt Fork of the Brazos by a large party that included vigilantes, a detail of Fort Griffin soldiers, and Tonkawa trackers. The vigilantes were escorting two notorious horse thieves and a man named George Causey. They had apprehended all three at Causey's camp between Little Duck and Stinking Creeks. White, well known and respected in Fort Griffin, where he was called "The Boss Hunter," vouched for Causey, saying he was a buffalo hunter

Buffalo hunter Frank Collinson recalled seeing victims of the Tin Hat-Band Brigade hanging from trees. Courtesy of the Panhandle-Plains Historical Museum, Canyon, Tex.

from Kansas and not a horse thief. The vigilantes released Causey, but, after spending the night at Collinson and White's camp, pulled out at dawn with the other two prisoners. Some time afterward, Tonkawa Johnson, leader of the Indian trackers, told Collinson the fate of those prisoners: "Maybe so white man cut 'um," he said, drawing his thumb across his throat. Collinson came across the body of one of the men a year later. "The skin on the neck was dry like old leather, but it showed plainly where the throat had been cut," he said.[76]

During that winter of 1876–77 John R. Cook, another buffalo hunter, rode into Albany to look up Sheriff Larn and ask his advice regarding a dispute over the ownership of a mare. He found the sheriff in T. E. Jackson's store conversing with cattleman Eugene "Cap" Millett, who was notorious for hiring outlaws as ranch hands and increasing his herds by dubious means. After hearing Cook's story, Larn and Millett both advised him to keep the mare in his possession "for want of better proof of the validity of the bill of sale."[77] Cook acted on the counsel and perhaps never saw the irony of seeking advice regarding a livestock dispute from men who would themselves become infamous in Texas for shady dealings in livestock.

CHAPTER SEVEN

1877: Enter the Texas Rangers

"Larn . . . was apparently a polished gentleman to meet, but he was meaner than a bed full of piss ants."

JOHN MEADOWS

Brothers Eugene, Alonzo, and Hiram Millett, known by the cattlemen of Texas as "Cap," "Lon," and "Hi," were Confederate veterans who had returned to their home in Guadalupe County, Texas, after the Civil War to find thousands of cattle running wild after four years of neglect. The Milletts were among the first to begin rounding up unbranded longhorns and driving them to northern markets at the Kansas railheads. In 1874 the Milletts moved a herd of six thousand cattle to rangeland in Baylor County, just north of Throckmorton, and began building what would become the biggest ranch in north Texas. In the spring of 1876 they constructed a fortresslike headquarters building near Miller Creek, a mile north of the Brazos River and right on the Western Cattle Trail to Dodge City, Kansas. The brothers became notorious for hiring outlaws and gunfighters as ranch hands and encouraging them to augment the Millett stock holdings by cutting out steers from northbound herds.

"There wasn't anybody but a rustler or gunman could get work with them," said A. P. Black, who himself rode for the ranchers. "The Milletts were a tough outfit straight through and hired the toughest bunch of men I ever ran up against. They even paid bonuses to their cowpunchers for every cow or horse they stole."[1]

As Don Biggers put it, "when a man got so tough he couldn't affiliate with civilization he would go to this [Millett] ranch and get a job."[2]

Jim McIntire, who worked cattle in north Texas and later became a Texas Ranger, came to know the Milletts and their range hands well. The brothers "would not hire a man unless he was a fighter," he said. "They did a lot of shady work and needed good men to execute their plans in raiding the ranges for stray cattle."[3]

In late 1876 a bunch of the hardcase Millett hands working the southern reaches of the Millett range took winter quarters at the ruins of the Old Stone Ranch. The deserted building was situated on Walnut Creek in southwestern Throckmorton County, about twelve miles west of Fort Griffin and some five miles from the Larn ranch. The Millett foreman in charge was a big, powerfully built man named Billy Bland. An experienced cowman and trail driver, Bland was said to be the first man to drive a herd from Texas to the Dakotas.[4] In 1875 he took part in one of the largest northern cattle drives on record when the Milletts, Seth Mabry, John O. Dewees, and James F. Ellison combined their herds and sent over one hundred thousand longhorns up the Chisholm Trail to the Kansas cattle towns.[5]

Newton J. Jones went to work for the Milletts in September 1876, helping brand almost three thousand head of cattle Bland had driven in from south Texas. It was Jones who recorded the details of Bland's story. Jones said Bland was searching for new range, and it was generally understood among the cowboys that when he found a good ranch location he and the Milletts would conclude a lease agreement in which Bland would run the cattle for five years on shares with the brothers.[6] This arrangement was similar to the agreement John Larn signed with J. M. Goff that same November of 1876, and may well have served the same purpose of hiding rustled cattle from the rightful owners.

Among the Millett hands wintering with Bland at the Old Stone Ranch were J. C. "Charley" Reed, Jack Lyons, Billy Gray, and Whit Vick. Sheriff John Larn and his shadow, Old John Selman, began frequenting the place and joining in the carousals that included much tipping of the bottle and trading stories of range adventures and saloon dustups.[7] Selman could hold his own in the drinking bouts, but apparently Larn held fast to his abstinence policy. John Meadows, who was employed by Larn at this time, said the man did not know what whiskey tasted like.[8] That winter Larn grew especially close to Billy Bland, a man much like himself, a natural-born leader who drew attention and commanded respect wherever he went, an expert cattleman, and a man totally without scruples.

On January 17, 1877, Bland and Charley Reed extended one of their sprees by a visit to The Flat. They rode into Fort Griffin, left their horses at the Clampett wagon yard, and began a tour of the town's ten saloons. As they emerged from one deadfall, Phin Reynolds ran into them and later recalled:

> Bill Bland, a foreman of the Millett outfit, struck me on the street at Fort Griffin and invited me to go with him that night and do some nightlife in the town. I told him that I could not as I was on my way to Weatherford. He said, "Stay over, Red," as he called me, "and we will have one hell of a time." But I refused, telling him I had to be on my way.[9]

Reynolds ever after was glad he turned down the invitation because before the night was over Bland did indeed have "one hell of a time."

He and Reed headed for the Bee Hive Saloon and Dance Hall, Fort Griffin's best-known resort. Opened originally by Owen Donnelly[10] and Patrick Carroll, saloonmen from Dallas, the Bee Hive was managed in 1877 by John H. Shanssey, a former pugilist and a veteran of boom camp sporting districts from Wyoming to Texas. Constructed of adobe brick and twice the size of most of its competitors, the Bee Hive featured a saloon in a large front room and a dance hall in the rear. It was, Frank Collinson said, "the most famous frontier saloon that ever graced or disgraced a town."[11] A large bee hive was pictured over the doorway with an invitation:

Within this Hive we are alive;
Good whisky makes us funny.
Get your horse tied, come inside,
And taste the flavor of our honey.[12]

Having tasted a great deal of that honey, Billy Bland and Charley Reed decided it would be "funny" to unlimber their six-shooters and shoot up some of the glassware behind the bar. When saloonkeeper Shanssey objected, they defied him or any lawman to try to interfere with their sport. Shanssey sent a messenger for Deputy Sheriffs William R. "Bill" Cruger and John M. Bogart, assigned to The Flat by Sheriff Larn. Both officers came running, followed by County Attorney Robert A. "Bob" Jeffress and a number of others drawn to the scene of excitement.

As Jeffress later related the story to his son, he approached Bland, "a big man, the biggest he had ever seen," and spoke quietly with him. Bland appeared to calm down, and then he said, "You seem like a pretty good fellow—have a drink." Jeffress declined, but accepted a cigar, and it looked like the crisis was over. Jeffress walked to the entrance of the back room where the dancing had resumed.

But at the bar Reed began to needle Bland, saying "the judge"— Jeffress—had talked the big foreman right out of his fun. This remark enraged Bland, who jerked out his pistol again and began blasting, shooting out the lights. Reed, Cruger, Jeffress, and perhaps others joined in the cannonade. Bedlam reigned as patrons, gamblers, and dancehall girls tumbled out of the building through doors and windows. When the shooting stopped, Shanssey got a lantern, and he and others crept back into the smoke-filled saloon.

They found a shambles. Among the casualties were two innocent bystanders. A young man named Dan Barrow, recently married, had taken a shot in the center of the forehead and died instantly.[13] Another random bullet hit J. W. Myers, the former army lieutenant turned lawyer who had attended the Democratic convention in Dallas with John Larn the previous year. He died two hours later.

Billy Bland was gut-shot; a bullet struck him about four inches below the navel and passed out through the small of his back. Members of the crowd carried him to Hank Smith's hotel where he writhed in agony and begged to be shot and put out of his misery before finally expiring.[14]

Bill Cruger was wounded only slightly, but Bob Jeffress, shot twice in the chest, once over the heart and once below it, was given no chance to live. Someone looked at him and said, "Take him out in the horse lot and open a fresh bale of hay and lay him on it. He can't last." But, against all odds, Jeffress did survive.[15]

Charley Reed escaped without a scratch and ran to the Clampett wagon yard, but was afraid to mount his horse because of the large crowd forming. Crawling over a back fence, he sneaked out of town and walked twelve miles to the Millett cow camp. There he told the story of the night's horrors to Newt Jones. In his version, Bland had been shooting in the saloon "just for fun," and Cruger gunned him down without warning. In retaliation, Reed returned the fire and wounded Cruger. Reed said when someone yelled at him, "I order you to surrender," he answered, "I order you to get," and the man got. He did not know who shot Barrow, Myers, and Jeffress.

With provisions, a saddle horse, and a pack animal provided by the Millett cowboys, Reed rode out of the Clear Fork country.[16]

The shootings in the Bee Hive had Fort Griffin in an uproar. At a well-attended public meeting the next day, a committee presided over by land promoter George A. Kirkland passed resolutions deploring "the sad results attending the conflict . . . between the Sheriff posse and opposing parties, [extending] sympathies to the families and friends of the deceased, [and commending] Deputy Sheriffs W. R. Cruger and J. M. Bogart [for] their determined effort in enforcing the laws." The committee directed Secretary J. Wallack to provide copies of the resolutions to Cruger and Bogart and to newspapers in Weatherford, Dallas, and Fort Worth.[17]

Sheriff John Larn, however, took no pleasure or pride in the actions of his deputies. He believed Charley Reed's version of the Bee Hive shootings—that Cruger had shot and killed his friend, Billy Bland, without warning. Bitter over the affair, Larn from that point on deliberately distanced himself from the law-and-order element. No longer would he ride with the Tin Hats. Bill Cruger, his own deputy, became his sworn enemy. Larn and his sidekick Selman increasingly associated with the outlaws and desperadoes with whom they felt more comfortable. That winter they spent long hours at the Old Stone Ranch, "acting in general like bad men do," as Newt Jones put it. There they and their desperado pals discussed ways to avenge Bland's death and hatched new schemes for rustling cattle.[18]

A killing involving Larn occurred that spring on the streets of Fort Griffin. Details are meager, for the only contemporary account appeared in the pages of the *Galveston Daily News*, quoting a Shackelford County correspondent. "A letter from Fort Griffin informs us of another tragedy at that place," said the *News* in its edition of March 7, 1877.

> The sheriff, John M. Larn, having received a capias from Collin county for the arrest of one John Hampton, proceeded to execute the writ, having first summoned another man

to assist him. Walking up to within a few feet of Hampton, the sheriff asked if that was his name. He replied, "Yes, by God, it is." The sheriff then informed him that he had a capias for his arrest, whereupon Hampton drew his pistol, and within a minute afterwards the firing became general. Hampton only succeeded in firing once, owing to a defect in his pistol, and soon received three fatal shots, from which he soon expired. The conduct of the sheriff was commended by all the citizens.

Several chroniclers of Fort Griffin violence, including two who were in the area at the time, have recounted the story of the shooting. Although details, including the name of the slain man, differ in these accounts, the narrators all agree that John Selman was the one summoned by Larn to assist in the arrest, and that it was he who delivered the fatal shots.

Edgar Rye wrote that Larn received a warrant for the arrest of one "Shorty" Collins, characterized by Rye as a trail hand and "an all-around horse thief, crook and murderer." Larn and Selman confronted Collins in The Flat as he caroused with some other drovers. Warrant in hand, Sheriff Larn ordered Collins to throw up his hands and consider himself under arrest. "Like a flash, 'Shorty's' hand dropped to the handle of his gun; at the same second Sillman [sic] sent a bullet crashing through 'Shorty's' left breast, and he fell dead at the sheriff's feet." Rye said the victim's companions were infuriated, but Larn and Selman, by "a quick, determined stand with their six-shooters in the face of the enraged cowpunchers," and some calm words of reason from the sheriff, defused the tense situation.[19]

In yet another account of the incident, Don H. Biggers wrote that Selman shot and killed a man named "Hampton" when the sheriff and his deputy attempted to arrest him. Hampton

walked directly toward the deputy, but made no attempt to draw a gun or make an assault. It is said that he was partially

deaf and failed to throw up his hands when commanded to
do so. The deputy began to shoot and when his pistol was
emptied the man fell, whereupon the deputy exultantly offered to bet a hundred dollars that he could cover every one
of the holes with a silver dollar. As only one ball had hit the
man the deputy would have won. The incident didn't even
call for a coroner's inquest.[20]

It was Frank Collinson's recollection that the man Selman killed
was a buffalo hunter, whose name Collinson could not recall. In
this version, the man got drunk and rowdy in Fort Griffin and loudly boasted about what he would do to the sheriff if he interfered
with his hell-raising. Informed of the threats, Larn and Selman confronted the troublemaker. Larn ordered him to raise his hands, but
when the hunter reached for his gun instead, Selman shot him.
Collinson said the body was unceremoniously dumped into a goods
box and buried behind a dance hall. "Digging the grave and bury-
ing the would-be bad man took less than an hour," he remembered.[21]

John Meadows, who knew Selman when he lived in the Clear
Fork country and also years later when he lived in El Paso, said that
of the twenty or more who died at Selman's hands, only two were
killed in fair fights. One was a man named Southerland in the 1870s
and the other was Deputy U.S. Marshal Baz Outlaw at El Paso in
1894.[22] "Southerland" may have been the man called "Shorty
Collins" by Rye and "John Hampton" by Biggers and the *Galveston
Daily News* correspondent. No other report of a gunfight and killing
involving John Selman during these years has come to light. Leon
Metz, an assiduous biographer of Selman, makes no mention of
Southerland.

Although—according to the Galveston newspaper correspondent—the conduct of the officers in the Hampton shooting met
with general approval in Fort Griffin, there may have been criti-
cism directed at the sheriff following the affair. At any rate, only a

few days later, Larn, who had been stewing since the Bee Hive shootings two months before, formally quit his job as Shackelford County sheriff, the resignation to take effect on March 20.[23] The county commissioners one week later appointed William R. Cruger, a twenty-eight-year-old native of Albany, Georgia, to replace him.

Cruger would play a vital role in Larn's final days. Most Clear Fork citizens held Bill Cruger in high regard and praised him for dispatching Billy Bland.[24] Like his predecessor, Cruger was a leading member of the Tin Hat-Band Brigade, and, also like Larn, he remained active in the organization after assuming the sheriff's office. A story circulated that on one occasion when he was eating with his prisoners, a party of vigilantes appeared and demanded several of them. Cruger, it is said, turned them over and continued with his meal.[25]

Now that Larn no longer wore a star or rode with the vigilantes, the desperadoes congregating at the Old Stone Ranch felt unprotected. They became increasingly apprehensive that the Tin Hats were preparing to move against them. Some began sleeping in the hills at night. The Millett cattle were ignored. Concerned, Lon Millett called on leaders of the vigilance committee, negotiated a deal, and presented it to the toughs at the ranch. Considering that Bland was dead and Reed had left the area, the Tin Hats agreed to let the others alone if they ceased their carousing and threats of vengeance. Most of the Millett cowboys accepted the terms, but a few particularly bitter malcontents such as Jack Lyons and Billy Gray refused. Following Charley Reed's lead, they mounted up and left the region.[26]

As part of the agreement, it appears that John Larn and John Selman were offered an inducement to end their conspiring with the Millett cowboys. On April 28 Shackelford County officials appointed them both deputy inspectors of hides and animals. Two of the most prominent men in the county, Joseph B. Matthews and Frank E. Conrad, co-signed their bonds in the amount of $1,000 each.[27] Duties of the office included inspection of all cattle entering

and leaving the county and supervision of butchers, who were required to submit a quarterly report to the Commissioners' Court
listing all animals that had been butchered. As proof of the validity of their reports, butchers had to retain the hides for inspection.[28]
This last provision would be a serious source of embarrassment for
John Larn before another year had passed.

Confronting tough, gun-packing trail drivers and demanding
that their herds be inspected could be dangerous work. Inspectors
Larn and Selman sought the help of Texas Rangers, who, on April
1, had established a camp on Elm Creek in Throckmorton County, about twenty miles from Fort Griffin. Lt. George W. Campbell
commanded Company B, Frontier Battalion, which had been ordered to the new location from a former campsite in Young County. Maj. John B. Jones, in command of the Frontier Battalion,
wanted Rangers closer to the Western Cattle Trail and the raucous
town of Fort Griffin. Later Campbell would move again, to a location he called Camp Sibley that was only eight miles from The Flat.
Ranger reports for May include several references to assistance ren-
dered to the Shackelford County cattle inspectors.[29]

According to John Meadows, the cattle inspection positions
proved to be lucrative for Larn and Selman. Meadows claimed the
inspectors regularly shook down trail drivers for $75 to $100 dollars
to allow their herds through.[30]

Trail boss Bob Lauderdale was working a herd north on the
Western Trail that spring. When he struck Fort Griffin he went looking for Larn.

> I walked into a saloon [and inquired for] the cattle inspector
> for trail herds, John Lauren by name. He was sitting on the sa-
> loon counter with his legs crossed and his feet drawn up under
> him. . . . He said, "Yes, I am the fellow you are looking
> for." . . . I told him whose cattle I was driving and where to
> find them and me. He said, "I will come out in the morning
> and look the herd over." The next morning I threw the cattle

out on the trail so they would string out and when Lauren got
there and rode through he said, "I see you have your own
brand on a few." I told him there were some we had missed
when we were branding and had to do it later. He said, "Well,
they do not belong on this range nohow. Hell! All I want is
the money anyway." So we did not turn the fresh brands
loose.[31]

During this period Larn continued to deal in property and livestock. On February 19, 1877, he paid John Selman $250 for addi-
tional cattle. On March 7 he purchased another batch from James
and Nathan Johnson, paying $721; Selman witnessed the transac-
tion.[32] In May he bought the 160-acre homestead adjoining his own
from M. F. Barber, paying $300 for it, and three days later sold one
of his Fort Griffin lots to storekeeper and realtor "Cheap John"
Marks for $100.[33]

Fort Griffin's reputation as the toughest town in Texas was becoming even more widespread at this time. A Texas newspaper in
1877 said that in The Flat, "Sharp's rifle and Colt's six-shooter are
the supreme law of the land, [but] among the roughs, thieves and
outlaws there is a class of good men . . . endeavoring to check the
lawlessness, and at their own expense have employed a marshal to
assist the regular officers in keeping order."[34]

The enforcer hired by the businessmen of Fort Griffin was
William C. "Big Bill" Gilson, former city marshal at Jacksboro, a
member of the Tin Hat-Band Brigade, and a staunch friend and
supporter of John Larn. At 225 pounds, toting "his little gun which
he knows so well how to use," he was a formidable figure.[35] Edgar
Rye described that "little gun" as "a sawed-off shotgun mounted
on a pistol handle, . . . loaded with buckshot and capable of deadly execution at short range."[36]

The Texas Rangers of Company B at nearby Camp Sibley actively assisted Marshal Gilson and Sheriff Cruger in law enforcement that summer. In June Cpl. T. W. Jones and three other

Rangers were sent to Fort Griffin on detached service "to assist the sheriff in enforcing the law."[37] In July Sheriff Cruger and twelve Rangers under the command of Sgt. J. E. Hines rode north to the Millett ranch in search of wanted men reportedly working for the Milletts. Later in the month a squad under Cpl. C. M. Sterling arrested two men in Fort Griffin for disturbing the peace and "Monte Jack" for escaping jail. Rangers apprehended six other jail breakers on the prairie and turned them over to Sheriff Cruger. Lt. Campbell's "Report of Scouts" for July contains an interesting notation that on the 16th, Sgt. Hines and Sheriff Cruger pursued "a horse thief by the name of Selman" for thirty miles but were unable to capture him.[38] This could not have been John Selman, who was very much available, but may have been his younger brother Tom Cat, who seems to have made himself scarce in the area about this time. In August, Ranger details under Corporal Sterling and Sgt. L. C. Knight patrolled The Flat and assisted City Marshal Gilson in arrests of several unruly characters, including longtime prostitutes Lou Baker and Anna Long.[39]

All the increased activity of municipal, county, and state lawmen to control outlawry was evidently not enough, for the vigilantes and the Tin Hat-Band Brigade went into action again. In August "a man named Monte [probably the jailbreaker 'Monte Jack' arrested by the Rangers in July], while being conveyed from Fort Griffin to Brownwood jail, was taken from the deputy sheriff by a party of masked men and hung to a tree and placarded: 'Beware of horse thieves.'"[40]

The *Austin Weekly Statesman* noted in September that "they make no more to-do about hanging men out at Fort Griffin than would naturally arise from the killing of so many bears. The vigilance committee pursued and hung three horse thieves to one tree three or four weeks ago, within a short distance of town, and the same committee lately started off on another lynching excursion."[41]

In a letter to Major Jones, Lieutenant Campbell reported that on September 28 Sheriff Cruger and City Marshal Gilson, while en route from Fort Griffin to Albany with a man in custody, were beset by "a mob of twelve men [who took] the prisoner away from them and hung him."[42]

Having fallen out with the vigilante crowd, Larn and Selman did not participate in this latest outbreak of Tin Hat activity, but a notorious frontier character known as "Hurricane Bill" became deeply involved with the night riders at this time.

William A. "Hurricane Bill" Martin, Indian fighter, buffalo hunter, desperado, gunfighter, and inveterate horse thief, was well known throughout Indian Territory, Kansas, Texas, New Mexico, and Arizona. A Texas fugitive list described him as a big man, six feet tall, weighing two hundred pounds, with light hair, blue eyes, and a "rather sharp" face, who generally presented a neat appearance and a "fine address."[43] At an early age he had been tagged with the nickname "Hurricane Bill" because of his penchant for spinning tall tales or "windies." Martin first showed up at Fort Griffin in the fall of 1875 as an army scout. He was in and out of the town during its boom period, gambling, carousing, and consorting with a prostitute named Jessie Tye, who was soon so identified with him that she became known in The Flat as "Hurricane Minnie" Martin.

Fort Griffin old-timer Sam Baldwin remembered Hurricane Minnie as being very attractive, a little stout, "but not overly so." He thought she was undoubtedly "the best looking woman around Fort Griffin."[44] In May 1876 the notorious horse thief and infamous harlot were legally united in holy wedlock, but, in a remarkable declaration to the Texas Rangers two years later, Martin would claim that the marriage had been forced upon him by the vigilantes.[45]

Although he never abandoned his career in horse thievery, Hurricane Bill greatly respected and feared the Shackelford vigilance committee and was careful to carry on his criminal work far from the Clear Fork. "Bill never stole any horses near Griffin," Frank Collinson recalled. "Like a wise old wolf he hunted a long way from his den."[46]

During Hurricane Bill's extended absences from The Flat, any loneliness that Hurricane Minnie may have felt was assuaged by John Selman.

The friends and partners—John Larn and John Selman—so alike in their rapacity and absolute lack of respect for human life, were nonetheless complete opposites in other aspects of moral conduct. Larn, who did not swear, smoke, or drink, was, by all accounts, devoted to his wife and child, and was never known to consort with the prostitutes of Fort Griffin. Selman, however, who also had a wife and children, practiced all the vices, including dalliance with prostitutes—especially Hurricane Minnie.

The consequence of this basic contrast in moral behavior between Larn and Selman provides one of the great ironies of their story. In the final showdown, when the Clear Fork citizenry turned viciously on the partners, Selman's licentious dalliance with Hurricane Minnie would lead to his salvation, whereas Larn, the straight-arrow family man, would be doomed.

Hurricane Bill was often arrested in Fort Griffin for gambling, pimping, and public drunkenness. He also got into several shooting scrapes. Frank Collinson recalled one fracas between Hurricane Bill and Jim White, the famous buffalo hunter, in which White put a bullet through Hurricane Bill's arm.[47] That injury did little to quell Bill's fighting, however. A former partner in White's hide-hunting business, Mike O'Brien, had opened a saloon in The Flat called The Hunter's Retreat. It was outside this establishment that he and Hurricane Bill Martin engaged in a memorable shoot-out.

Following a drunken argument in the saloon, Martin declared he was "going to clean up on" O'Brien, staggered across the street to the picket shanty he shared with Hurricane Minnie, and took up position at a window with his rifle. "He hollered at somebody to tell Mike to come out the door," an eyewitness recalled.

When Mike stepped out on the street with a Winchester, Hurricane Bill blazed away at him. And Mike went in and got his

buffalo gun and stick and set it down. And they shot at one
another until I guess Bill got excited and most of his bullets
went wild. And he was afraid of killing Mike, too, that is,
afraid of that Vigilance Committee. . . . Yes, they was shooting at each other, and Mike hollered to his bartender inside:
"Bring me a drink here!" And the bartender poured out a
glass of whiskey and a glass of water and walked out there
with them while Mike was sitting there and Bill was banging
away at him. Old Mike had lots of gall.[48]

Responding to this drunken gunplay, City Marshal Gilson attempted to arrest Hurricane Bill. According to Edgar Rye, he literally ran into him in another saloon. Martin was on his way out
the door, pistol in hand, as Gilson came in, carrying his formidable
sawed-off shotgun. The two collided and "Bill's pistol was discharged so close to the marshal's face that the flash powder-burned
his eyes, and 'Old Betsey,' the marshal's gun, tore a hole in the ceiling of the saloon."[49]

On October 19, 1876, Martin was indicted for assault with intent to murder. He made bond of $1,000, partly posted by two men
friendly to him—John Selman and J. Hunt Kelly, a neighbor of
Selman's on the Clear Fork. When the case was called on April 18,
1877, Martin failed to appear. He was still missing the following
October and the bond was forfeited.[50]

Four months later, on February 19, 1878, Hurricane Minnie
signed over her furnished house in Fort Griffin to Selman. Perhaps
this was Old John's way of recouping his lost investment in Martin.[51]

The story is murky and details are few, but apparently the Tin
Hat-Band Brigade had enlisted the outlaw and reprobate Hurricane Bill Martin to help them in their campaign against other outlaws. The vigilantes probably used Martin as a guide to lead them
to the hideouts of horse thieves. Buffalo hunter Skelton Glenn later
claimed that on these forays Hurricane Bill was the rope man, with

the responsibility of tying up victims and cutting them down after the grisly work was completed. Glenn said that the vigilantes paid Martin a fee for this work, and he was allowed to keep whatever of value he could take from the bodies.[52]

Larn and Selman, no longer riding with the Tin Hats, concentrated on their ranch activities in 1877. John Meadows, employed by them that year, was in a position to know how they operated. What he saw appalled him. He developed a bitter hatred for both men that was still forcefully expressed in interviews conducted sixty years later.

About the first of March 1876, Meadows came off the buffalo ranges, where he had been hunting, to take a job as a cowhand for Larn and Selman, men he would later characterize as "two of the damnedest, meanest, dirtiest thieves ever in Texas." He claimed they tried to get him into cow stealing, so he quit the job after a few months.[53]

However, he hired on with the partners again the following year. He never explained why he went back but said he always regretted it. Larn and Selman were guilty of many atrocious crimes, Meadows alleged, including the theft of a cattle herd and the murder of its owners.

As Meadows told the tale, the Clear Fork partners had arranged to purchase a bunch of cattle brought from Indian Territory by two young men. Delivery was to be made at a place called Bottomless Wells, two sinkholes on the right-hand prong of Tecumseh Creek. At the meeting, however, Larn and Selman paid for the herd, not with cash, but with bullets. They killed both young men and threw their weighted bodies into the Bottomless Wells.

"My God," said Meadows, "one of these come up. It had a rock tied to it, but it had swelled up and floated up to the top, and them was the two boys that they bought them cattle from and didn't pay them. I seen the body of one of them boys. That was in '77."[54]

Meadows relished telling another story of how Larn and Selman got euchred by their own kind. The partners had moved a herd of stolen cattle to the vicinity of Flat Top Mountain in the winter of 1876–77. "There they did their dirty work themselves," burning altered brands. "Next spring Millett's outfit went in there, and they just cleaned Larn and Selman up. They took every damn thing that was burnt. . . . They went in there and cut them cattle and brought them home. . . . They would have had trouble if Larn had been there."[55]

John Meadows hated both Larn and Selman passionately and had difficulty deciding which man was worse. Larn, the smarter of the two, was "apparently a polished gentleman to meet, but he was meaner than a bed full of piss ants."[56] Meadows never heard him use vulgar or profane language; "dadgummit" was the worst word in his vocabulary. Larn "was originally from Alabama, where all the damn rascals come from," said Meadows, who himself was an Alabaman. "He didn't think [about] anything, only killing, but he'd kill you in a minute and take any old chance to get to do it."[57]

Meadows considered Selman "one of the dirtiest men" he ever knew. "There was nothing on earth too low for him to do." Larn, he believed, "had a little principle, but Selman had none at all whatever. He was close to a six-shooter. I believe I'd rather fight Larn twice than Selman once. He took the advantage every time."[58] Selman was "the meanest of the two. He was the meanest man that ever lived."[59]

While working for the partners, Meadows had built up over $300 in back pay, which, he claimed, they refused to give him. So he determined to kill them both. Armed with a double-barreled shotgun loaded with sixteen goose-shot on each side, he selected a bushwhack location, a site on Lambshead Creek along a route he expected Larn and Selman to follow. But before he could carry out his plan, J. Hunt Kelly, with whom he was living, intervened. "I picked up this gun and started across that corn field, and Uncle Hunt overtook me," Meadows said. "He took me and carried me back. By God, I never was so mad. . . . I wanted to kill them men."[60]

John P. Meadows, who hated Larn and Selman passionately and with good reason, started out across a cornfield with a shotgun to kill them both, but was restrained by J. Hunt Kelly.

CHAPTER EIGHT

1878: Fear Grips the Clear Fork

"A feud has existed here for several months between Jhn. M. Lau-ren, Jhn. H. Sellman & party and the farmers on account of the unlawful killing and using of stock. . . ."

TEXAS RANGER SERGEANT J. E. VAN RIPER

John Larn continued to play the role of respectable, hard-working rancher and family man, and, despite the growing suspicion among his neighbors that at his core he was the antithesis of respectability, some in the Fort Griffin country still defended him. The confusion was understandable. People found it hard to believe that a man so devoted to his family and so affable and courteous in manner and speech with his neighbors could be capable of criminal behavior and brutality. The man's complex personality perplexed many, including John C. Irwin, who had a small spread not far from Larn's place, and was acutely aware of the bloody work that had been attributed to his neighbor since the Bush Knob Massacre of 1873.

One morning Irwin watched in disbelief as Larn calmly cut out some cows from Irwin's grazing herd and drove them off. His knowledge of Larn's mankilling reputation prevented him from protesting. The two men met in Fort Griffin a few days later, and Larn inquired how things were going with his neighbor. Not so good, Irwin admitted. Drought had destroyed most of his grass and he had no money to buy feed for his cattle.

Larn threw an arm around Irwin's shoulders. "I'll tell you what I am going to do," he said, smiling. "I am going to give you $100 just to help you along."

Irwin accepted the money. Both men knew the value of the cattle Larn had stolen greatly exceeded $100 but this was cold cash and with it Irwin could purchase some grain for his remaining stock. He was grateful. "Somehow," he said, "I never could dislike Larn after that."[1]

Late in 1877 John Larn had secured a contract to provide one to three cows a day to feed the soldiers and Tonkawa Indians at Fort Griffin. It soon became apparent to his neighbors, however, that even as Larn fulfilled his contract his herds never seemed to diminish. "Larn just depended on downright stealing, and that is all that there was to it," John Meadows said. "He had a contract to feed them Tonkawa Indians at Fort Griffin, . . . and, by God, he stole so damn many of his neighbors' cattle that they couldn't stand it any longer."[2]

New rumors of thievery and murder attributable to Larn and Selman became widespread in the early months of 1878. Meadows heard the tales as far away as Hemphill County in the northern panhandle of Texas, where he was riding the W. S. Ikard range along the Washita River. One of the most frequently repeated was the story of the stone masons.

Larn had employed two men to build a rock fence around his property and reportedly had given them $100 in advance. The balance of $400 was to be paid upon completion of the job. But when the fence was finished the men disappeared without a trace. The suspicion spread that Larn had disposed of them.[3] Meadows, who had been working for Larn when the masons started the fence but left before they finished, was quick to believe the worst: "The way [Larn] paid them was to shoot them and throw them in the Clear Fork."[4]

It was true that in the spring of 1878, some time after the workmen disappeared, a badly decomposed body was pulled from the river at Fort Griffin. Despite its condition, a friend of the masons thought he recognized the corpse as one of them. Frank Collinson remembered this man's name as "Tom Kinkade."[5] Several Texas Rangers viewed the body and thought they saw evidence of foul play, but a jury led by Coroner Edgar Rye declared the death due to accidental drowning.[6]

Later, another body, believed to be that of the second man, was discovered downstream in Stephens County. Later still, when Larn and Selman were no longer terrorizing the Clear Fork country, two witnesses reportedly admitted having direct knowledge of their employer's murder of the masons.[7]

John Meadows claimed Larn and Selman had previously committed a similar murder. A French carpenter, whose name Meadows remembered as "Old Chips" Bendenger, had worked on the houses of both men. When he was finished, according to Meadows, the partners killed him and tossed his body in the Clear Fork.[8]

Phin Reynolds was one of those who never accepted these stories. He said he had been told that a Clear Fork resident saw one of the missing stone masons long after the supposed murder. "Although Larn was a pretty hard character, I do not believe that he did [those murders]," Reynolds said in 1945. "I always liked John Larn personally."[9]

Like Irwin and Reynolds, others found it difficult to believe Larn was a vicious murderer. Members of the Matthews and Reynolds families, kin to Mary Jane, were particularly reluctant to accept the growing conviction among Clear Fork residents that they had a monster in their midst. Most of the Reynolds and Matthews clan thought it impossible that a sweet girl like Mary Jane could live with a brutal killer. Perhaps Larn blotted a few brands, but brand tampering was a practice more commonly employed by prominent Texas cattlemen than anyone cared to admit. The work of the outlaws hired by the Millett brothers up north was clear evidence of that. No doubt Larn had killed a few men—cattle rustlers like the Hayes outfit or horse thieves like the Watson gang—but cold-blooded murder to save a few dollars was something else entirely. John Larn was too much a gentleman to stoop to that level, they argued.

John Selman was a different matter altogether. After he had deliberately gunned down that cowboy on the streets of Fort Griffin, they believed Selman capable of anything—and he wasn't married to a daughter of the Reynolds-Matthews clan.

What the Larn defenders did not realize was that, more than anything else, it was the influence of John Larn that had turned Selman into a criminal and callous murderer, as he demonstrated many times after Larn was dead and buried.

Larn could not have been unaware of the growing tide of anger directed toward him, but with a display of incredible arrogance and audacity, in the early months of 1878 he actually increased his crimes against his neighbors. He particularly targeted those small farmers and stockmen, recently settled along the Clear Fork, who were derisively called "Grangers" by the established cattlemen.

For months he had fulfilled his government beef contract by stealing and slaughtering the animals of his neighbors. Most of his victims—peaceable folk completely intimidated by the likes of Larn and Selman—suffered their losses in silence. But in February a man named A. J. Lancaster, who claimed to have personally seen Larn and Selman butcher stolen cattle and throw the hides in the river, resolved to find solid evidence against the pair and bring them to justice. He and a few friends attempted to drag the river bottom for hides. They were at this work when Larn rode up, took in the situation at a glance, and called down from the riverbank: "Any man who pulls that line up will be a dead man." All work promptly ceased and the settlers went home.[10]

But Lancaster was a stubborn man and did not give up. He filed a formal complaint with the county authorities, charging Larn and Selman with theft of cattle and concealing evidence of their crimes. Justice of the Peace Edgar Rye issued a search warrant and directed Sheriff Cruger to investigate the matter. Well aware of the hazards involved in a direct confrontation with Larn and Selman, who represented almost a law unto themselves and were likely to fight if threatened, Cruger organized a large posse and called on the Texas Rangers for assistance in serving the warrant. Ranger Lt. G. W. Campbell and Pvt. Alex Hutchison joined the sheriff and a dozen possemen in a raid on the Larn ranch. John Irwin, a member of that posse, has left an account of what transpired:

> When we reached Larn's house, Lt. Campbell ordered us to halt while he went in and conferred with Larn and served his papers. He was in there an hour or so, and when he came out, Larn, John Selman, Selman's brother, and a man named Tom Curtis were with him. Larn started cursing our entire bunch of deputies and dared them to come through the yard. The Ranger remonstrated with him but to no avail. . . . We didn't go through the yard, but we did go around it and to the river just below his house, where we fished out cow hides with grappling hooks. This was done in the presence of Larn and the Selmans. Those hides had various brands on them, but we found none with the brands of either Selman or Larn. Larn claimed they had been planted there to frame him.[11]

Ranger Hutchison, however, did not remember a display of anger and defiance by Larn. Back at camp he told Newt Jones, who was by this time a Ranger in Company B, that when Campbell entered the house and announced he had a search warrant, "Larn offered to surrender his pistol to Campbell, but Campbell didn't take his gun, saying, 'I don't need to disarm you; I just came to see this place searched, and if you don't refuse that, I don't need to disarm you.'"[12]

In his report to Maj. John B. Jones of February 26, Lt. Campbell wrote: "Have had a big excitement in . . . making arrest of Jhn. M. Lauren [sic] and Jhn. Sillman [sic], charged with stealing cattle and killing them for beef. . . . Citizens swore out a search warrant and I served it and found six beef hides in the bed of the Clear Fork, none in their own brands. [I have] taken them to Fort Griffin and turned them over to the officers. A compromise was made and the parties were released."[13]

Ranger Hutchison later told Newt Jones that the brand on only one of the hides could be identified, and the animal's owner was offered fifty dollars by someone—evidently not Larn himself—to drop any charges.[14]

"Larn and Selman defied the Rangers and refused to be disarmed or arrested," alleged a story in a Texas newspaper. "They repaired to the magistrate's court armed and forcibly took away the principle witness from the court, and he soon left the country. For the want of this witness's evidence no information was filed. The hides were at the court to be examined, but from fear of the parties accused and witnesses gone the prosecution was abandoned."[15]

This version could not have been accurate because the chief witness against Larn and Selman was A. J. Lancaster, who did not leave the Clear Fork country but remained to play a key role in the ultimate defeat of Larn and company.

It is possible the case was dismissed because many important people in that area did not want to drag an unwilling John Larn into court. As a former vigilante leader, he knew too many secrets. He could name every prominent and influential man who had worn the Tin Hat and participated in the hangings. Larn knew— literally—where the bodies were buried. Testifying with his back against the wall in a court of law, he might begin talking and never stop until all of this came spewing out into the open. The public in Shackelford County was reluctant to indict and prosecute members of the Tin Hat-Band Brigade for their lethal operations, but anti-vigilante sentiment in other parts of the state could bring action by the governor, the adjutant general, and the Rangers.

At this juncture the volatile situation in the Clear Fork country was further exacerbated by the reappearance of Hurricane Bill Martin. Still a fugitive after jumping his bonds on the assault to murder charge pending against him, Martin was arrested in March at Castroville, Texas. Rangers under Capt. Lee Hall—acting on information received from Hunt Kelly, one of the fugitive's out-of-pocket bondsmen—took Martin into custody, jailed him at San Antonio, and notified Sheriff Cruger and Lieutenant Campbell of Company B.[16] Campbell sent Rangers J. E. Hines and E. W. Jordan to San Antonio, where they received the prisoner from Bexar County officers on March 24. They delivered Martin to Sheriff Cruger at Albany a week later.[17]

All the way from San Antonio Martin demonstrated to his Ranger guards how he got the name "Hurricane Bill." His wind blew long and hard as he regaled them with stories of the Shackelford County vigilantes and their ruthless deeds. He feared the Tin Hats far more than he feared the law, he said, but he offered to divulge even more information to Lieutenant Campbell about the clan's activities if the Rangers would assure his protection.

Campbell, an ambitious and courageous officer of the law, believed the vigilantes were a destructive law-defying element. He wanted it wiped out and its leaders brought to justice. Since moving into the area the previous year, Campbell had been investigating the Tin Hats with little success. He now leaped at Martin's offer, seeing the notorious outlaw as the key to revealing the mob. He assigned four Rangers to guard and protect Martin in the rude lockup at Albany and wrote a long letter to Major Jones, describing the situation in detail and calling for support. Martin, he said, had "spoken very plainly," admitting participation in the worst of [the mob's] cut-throat butcheries of killing and hanging . . . committed in the last four or five years. . . . He [wants] each and every one of these bloodthirsty and cut-throat "Tin-Hat" committee [members] to be checked in their murderous career and justice and punishment meted [out] to the full extent of the law. . . . He will give the names of . . . good and reliable citizens, . . . eye witnesses to . . . the atrocious and inhuman deeds performed by this Vigilance Committee. . . . He can himself show the skeletons of . . . seven victims of this terrible mob, foully murdered in the past few years. . . .

Martin is not a member of the clan but has been with them when they have done some of the killing. They have always been afraid he would tell on them, and they caucased on him three different times, causing him to marry a prostitute or leave the country, then again wanting to hang him for marrying her, but [he] was saved by three votes. . . .[18]

Martin gave specific information about a recent case. During a dispute over a card game at Rath City, buffalo hunter John Dougherty stabbed John Curry, alias "English Jack," to death. Dougherty was taken out and hanged almost immediately by a gang calling itself "The Hunters' Protective Union." J. M. Dougherty, the father of this latest mob victim and a neighbor of John Larn, vowed to hunt down his son's killers.[19] Martin told Ranger Hines that one of those killers was a leader of the Tin Hats and a current office holder in Shackelford County.[20]

Campbell said Martin offered to testify against the Tin Hats and provide more names at the next session of the district court, scheduled for April 15. In testifying, he sought no special consideration for himself, Martin insisted. He did not intend "to screen or protect himself in any way or to elude justice." His only motivation was a desire to see the vigilante members dealt with by the law, but he was fearful that he would be mobbed while in custody if the Tin

Hats learned of his testimony, and demanded the protection of the Rangers. He said others would also come forward to testify against the vigilantes if they were provided the same protection.

"I think that I can procure other witnesses who will give evidence in these cases that will corroborate [Martin's testimony]," Campbell told Jones. He named two of these "indispensable witnesses" as George Anderson, a former deputy sheriff of Shackelford County, and a Mrs. Harris, who could give testimony for the state "in the Kincade murder," presumably referring to the discovery of the body thought to be one of the stone masons allegedly murdered by John Larn.

To protect Martin, Campbell said he would continue to keep four Rangers at Albany, which still had no proper jail, but thirteen other men were also being held there on various charges. He requested from Major Jones a quick response to these revelations and said he hoped Jones could be present when the district court opened. "If anything is done, there will be no County Officers left to conduct Court," he said, implying that those officers would be accused by Martin of vigilante complicity and become defendants themselves. "I think that the parties, or at least the worst of them, can be arrested at the Court House, at the meeting of the Court if Martin will do what he says he will, and I have not the least doubt to suspicion else." Campbell stressed that it was imperative that secrecy be maintained. "No one has any suspicion of this, neither will they find out until we can secure them all."[21]

Secrecy was not maintained. Campbell posted his letter to Major Jones at Fort Griffin, and it was intercepted by vigilance committee leaders who recognized that this out-of-control Ranger lieutenant, if allowed to continue, was about to blow the lid off the community. Almost every man of substance and standing in the Clear Fork country had condoned, aided and abetted, or participated in the work of the vigilantes. Highly respected cattlemen Joseph Matthews and Barber Reynolds; their sons and sons-in-law; Frank Conrad, Charles Meyer, Hank Smith, John Shanssey, and other merchants

and businessmen of Fort Griffin and Albany; magistrates, sheriffs
and their deputies, and assorted other county officials, including
W. H. Ledbetter, Cornelius K. Stribling, Edgar Rye, Bill Cruger,
and James Draper had either ridden with the Tin Hat-Band
Brigade on its forays or had assisted it with contributions of horses,
guns and ammunition, provisions, or moral support.

By dealing with Hurricane Bill Martin, Campbell posed a threat
to the entire establishment of the area.

Martin's unsupported testimony in open court would no doubt
prove embarrassing to many, but an even greater concern of the
region's leaders was the possibility that Hurricane Bill's allegations
might be backed by John Larn and John Selman in a plea-bargain
agreement with Campbell. If that should happen, the case would
explode like a bombshell and criminal proceedings against the community leaders would certainly follow. Larn and Selman knew a
great deal more about Tin Hat activities than did Martin, and
Larn, especially, as a prosperous cattleman and former sheriff,
would be a much more impressive and persuasive witness than the
notorious horse thief, Hurricane Bill. To prevent that appalling possibility, Martin had to be muzzled and Campbell's ambitions
thwarted.

Judge J. R. Fleming of the Twelfth District Court was well aware
of this potential for disaster. When the court convened on April 15,
Hurricane Bill's assault case was on the docket. Campbell appeared
in court and tried to introduce Martin's explosive charges, but
Fleming refused to hear them. Campbell angrily demanded a
change of venue, but Fleming denied that request also and post-
poned further action on the case.

The grand jury, meeting shortly thereafter, heard testimony from
Throckmorton County residents who charged Larn and Selman
with butchering their cattle. One witness swore that he saw them
shoot and skin two cows and throw the hides in the river. Campbell
tried to get Hurricane Bill on the stand to provide further incriminating testimony, but the grand jury, led by its foreman, refused to

hear Martin and declined to bring indictments against Larn and Selman.[22]

On May 1, 1878, Judge Fleming moved to get rid of the pesky Lieutenant Campbell. He wrote Texas Governor R. B. Hubbard and reviewed the peculiar conditions prevailing in Shackelford County. "There has been a Vigilante Committee operating in that County and . . . I have used every [means] to find out the guilty parties," he said.

> Lt. Campbell also has been trying to flush them out. But he has been unfortunate in his choice of information. . . . A few weeks ago a desperado by the name of "Hurricane Bill" was arrested and is under guard in Albany. He is a man utterly devoid of principle and is now indicted [for attempting] to assassinate a man in that county. By some means he has per- suaded Campbell that he was one of the Committee and has given him the names of all the best citizens in the county as being in this organization. This fellow Hurricane Bill is in- terested in maligning and traducing the character of the good citizens of that county—and he can be impeached by the tes- timony almost of every man, woman and child in the county. . . .
>
> I was told by citizens then that Campbell was constantly in consultation with the man "Hurricane Bill" and believed everything he said. I don't know whether this is true or not but I know the general opinion of the people of the county is that [his reliance on Martin] destroys his usefulness in the public service at that place.

Fleming added that it was not his intent to make charges against Campbell. "As far as I know he has done his duty. The only thing that I would have censored him about was making an affidavit for change of venue in this case. I think it would have been better for him to attend to the duties of his office and let the defendant seek his remedy through citizens of the county as the statute provided he shall do." But the judge strongly recommended that Campbell and his command be transferred to some other county. "Should you desire further information," he said, "[I] refer you to good citizens in Shackelford County, at whose suggestion I write."[23]

Within a week the word came down to Major Jones from the office of Adjutant General William Steele: remove this trouble-making Ranger lieutenant from Shackelford County.

Jones moved swiftly. On May 7 he notified Campbell that Company B would be disbanded and that his service would no longer be required after the end of the month. All Rangers in the company were to be honorably discharged with the exception of a single squad. Those remaining would stay on at Camp Sibley to act as guides for a replacement company arriving some time in the future.[24]

The letter was confirmed on May 18 by Special Order Number 131, which officially disbanded the company as of May 31 and directed Campbell to issue discharges on that date, turn over all public property to Sgt. J. E. Van Riper and the five men who would remain, and then consider himself relieved from duty.[25]

Although members and supporters of the Shackelford County vigilance committee welcomed the news of Campbell's removal, the Grangers along the Clear Fork in Throckmorton County were dismayed. Campbell and the Rangers of Company B had been their protection from the depredations of John Larn and his followers. They wrote a desperate letter of protest to Major Jones and enclosed a petition urging him to reconsider his decision and come personally to the region and investigate the problems. To illustrate the serious nature of the affair, they sketched out the history:

"The citizens of this neighborhood have been missing stock, having suspected parties killing them. Got a warrant to search for the hides and found them in the river. . . . One of the men concerned in throwing the hides in the river [Larn] says he is captain of the vigilant committee. . . ."

With regard to Hurricane Bill they asked: "Has the grand jury the right to reject a prisoner from coming before them to give evidence against other parties as it was done last court?"

For further particulars they referred Major Jones to Lieutenant Campbell. They expressed alarm that Company B was to be disbanded, for they expected "serious trouble" when the Rangers departed "as there has been threats made to that effect. . . . Our stock and our lives are not safe." A number of Throckmorton County settlers, including A. J. Lancaster, H. R. and J. B. Treadwell, and William Brisky signed the letter.[26]

A few days later a telegram from two professional men of the region, medical doctor William Baird and dentist S. K. Smith, reiterated the plea to Major Jones: "Nine tenths of the people in this part of the country want Lieut. Campbell's company of Rangers retained here. A letter and petition to that effect will follow this."[27]

Maj. John B. Jones was highly respected, almost revered, in the northern counties of Texas for forming the Frontier Battalion of the Rangers and personally leading them in battle against marauding Indians in 1874. In the eyes of the people who lived in those frontier counties, Jones could be given as much credit, if not more, than the U.S. Army for the elimination of the Indian problem. The distraught Grangers of Throckmorton County believed that the Larn problem also would be resolved if Jones could be induced to appear on the scene.

During these weeks, fear ran rampant in the Clear Fork country.

The Grangers and small ranchers along the river lived in constant dread of a brutal retribution visited upon them by Larn and his henchmen. A newspaper reported that the Grangers "ceased to work their crops; kept close to their houses, and would not even go to their cowpens to milk; sending their wives out to transact all their business. . . . But few of them undressed themselves at night for two weeks for fear of an attempt to mob. They were trying to sell their places, to leave the country."[28]

Tin Hat-Band Brigade members and their supporters feared those who seemed about to inform on them. It was common knowledge that Hurricane Bill Martin was willing to tell all he knew about the nightriders, and rumors continued that Larn and Selman were negotiating with the Texas Rangers to cut a deal. It was said they had offered to identify and testify against vigilante committee members in return for the dropping of state charges against themselves. The rumors apparently had some basis in fact; Ranger "Newt" Jones later said Larn and Selman had scheduled a secret meeting with Sergeant Van Riper to reveal locations of the bodies of vigilante victims who had never been buried.[29]

With the Ranger guards removed, Martin and the other prisoners confined in the crude Albany lock-up were terrorized by the very real possibility that they would be visited one night by a party of masked men wearing tin in their hats and carrying a hangman's noose.

Even the few Texas Rangers remaining at Camp Sibley felt fear. As Sergeant Van Riper confirmed in a letter to Major Jones, Larn and his followers had threatened them and on at least one occasion had set up an ambush and attempted to carry out those threats.[30]

If he was not afraid, tough Old John Selman certainly felt uneasy. During this tense period he and Larn were themselves the targets of several bushwhack attempts. Once, Larn's hat was shot from his head, and on another occasion a shotgun blast from a hidden enemy tore the horn from Selman's saddle.[31] Deciding it was time to clear out of the Clear Fork country, on May 15 Old John sold all his cattle and twelve horses to Larn for $3,000 in cash.[32]

Only John Larn seemed unaffected by the fear gripping the countryside. The fact that he could pay Selman $3,000 in cash—a considerable amount of money in 1878—is evidence of his prosperity and ambition. He had come a long way toward attaining his goals of becoming a big and important cattleman. That he *would* purchase Selman's stock indicates that Larn had every intention of

staying right where he was. He was determined that his enemies
would not drive him out. He would drive them out.

As spring turned to summer along the Clear Fork of the Brazos,
John Larn—successful rancher, devoted husband and father—by
day tended to his home, his stock, and his family. But at night he led
his followers in sweeps through the countryside, destroying crops,
shooting down livestock, intimidating and terrorizing his neighbors.

Of course, John Selman rode with him. Having removed his fi-
nancial ties to the Clear Fork country, Selman was ready to cut and
run at a moment's notice, but he stayed on to side with Larn in his
campaign of terror. According to Texas Ranger reports, Larn led
a band of some sixteen men, all "armed with shot guns and improved cartridge guns."[33] In addition to the Selman brothers, Larn's
gang may have included Tom Curtis, John Gross, Jim Herrington,
a former Texas Ranger named Blue Roberts, and a man known
only as "Thistle."

Some Grangers simply gave in to the intimidation, pulled up
stakes, and moved out. For those who defied Larn and his gunmen,
there were death threats and assassination attempts. John C. Irwin
said that Larn openly threatened his life and on one occasion tried
to kill him.[34] Larn also openly attacked James Treadwell and shot
his horse out from under him.[35]

Although most of the Grangers who remained were not fighting
men by nature and experience, they refused to succumb to this kind
of thuggery. They organized and armed themselves to defend their
property and their lives.

On June 15, Sergeant Van Riper, in his first report to Major
Jones after assuming command of the skeleton Ranger force remaining at Camp Sibley, stressed the seriousness of the situation:

> A feud has existed here for several months between Jhn. M.
> Lauren, Jhn. H. Sellman & party and the farmers on account
> of the unlawful killing and using of stock, and finally the
> killing of stock in general of the farmers on the range and

elsewhere through malicious intents, and serious threats to exterminate and drive the farmers from the country; the farmers not being able to receive redress by law, have taken up arms in defense of their lives and property. Both parties travel the country in squads, well armed. Trouble is hourly expected.[36]

Van Riper considered the situation so explosive that he wrote a separate letter on the same day to his commander, providing more detail:

> Affairs in this section of the country . . . are in a terrible stage—armed parties of men continually riding the country—riding at midnight into the door yards of peaceable citizens and discharging their firearms, frightening women and children, citizens are being run out of the country, leaving their property. Mr. Treadwell and others living in the neighborhood of Jhn. M. Lauren and Jhn. H. Sellman are continually finding their horses and cattle shot down on the prairies. Milch cows and calves are shot down on the premises after night fall. [The Grangers] have recently lost several hundred dollars worth of stock in this manner. They have now taken up arms in defense of their lives and property, as a last resort, having received no redress nor encouragement by law. Both parties going to squads, serious trouble is hourly expected.

Van Riper said that he had been informed by "good and reliable authorities" that John Larn had made "heavy threats" against his enemies and had sworn "to have the lives of five certain men in this country." Two of the five, Van Riper was told, were Lieutenant Campbell and himself. He and Campbell, who still remained in the Ranger camp, took the reports very seriously and remained vigilant, expecting a raid at any time. There had been an unsuccessful attempt to ambush him a few nights before when he was bringing a prisoner from Fort Griffin to the Ranger camp, Van Riper said.

He, Campbell, and law-abiding citizens were "earnestly beseeching and praying" for Major Jones to come and see firsthand the gravity of the situation. Together they were "asking and praying for aid and protection from the dreadful crisis" in which they found themselves. "Something will have to be done," Van Riper said, "or this country will ere long be the scene of blackening crimes [too] horrible to think of."

Having discovered that some of Company B's reports had been removed from the post office at Fort Griffin by someone "closely connected by oaths and ties" to the troublemakers, Van Riper said he would mail his letter at Breckenridge, in Stephens County. He concluded by again imploring Jones to come at once and see for himself the deplorable state of affairs. He said he spoke for all the honest "citizens of this community who are being robbed of their rights and property, and denied the liberty of free people."[37]

Although he had been relieved from duty and no longer had any legal authority, Campbell had stayed on at Camp Sibley. If Major Jones came, Campbell wanted to be available to explain personally to him the deteriorating conditions in the Clear Fork country and the complexity of the crisis. On June 16 he wrote to Jones, adding his voice of concern. He repeated Van Riper's summary of the current situation, saying parties of heavily armed men continued to range the countryside and that bloody clashes were apt to erupt at any time. The Larn gunmen had been operating, he said, "in parties of from four to six men, at the dead hour of night, riding into the door yards of the settlers and firing off their guns around the doors. The settlers are so badly frightened. I learn to-day that several of them have left their homes, crops and property and have left the country entirely."

Campbell mentioned the two missing masons who had worked for Larn and the discovery of bodies believed to be theirs, adding: "This week another man, nearest neighbor to Mr. Lauren, has very mysteriously disappeared and has not been heard from up to this time."

Conditions had gone from bad to worse in the two weeks since Company B had been disbanded, Campbell said. During that time some $300 worth of stock had been killed or run off, and "scarcely a day passes without there being stock of some kind killed." Campbell said he felt a sense of personal responsibility to the honest citizens because during the weeks of the gathering storm he had consistently counseled them to be calm and wait for Major Jones to come and deal with the problem.

> I had the matter worked up so . . . you would see how it was, and take hold of it, and bring the guilty parties to justice. [The people] are after me every day wanting to know what to do, and when you will be up, as I had told them that if they would keep quiet until you arrived that the troubles would be stopped. You have no idea how bad your presence is needed here at the present time, and how the citizens look to you and will flock to you for relief. [The question] has been asked me fifty times when you will be up. I have been telling them not to be rash and get themselves in trouble.

Campbell told Jones he felt so strongly about his personal stake in the region's crisis that he intended to remain on duty without pay long enough to see the guilty parties ferreted out and brought to justice. "Until this thing is done," he said, "I am not satisfied."

Annoyed by the failure of Major Jones to appear at the scene of the troubles, Campbell was also distressed by stories circulating that he and the men of Company B had received dishonorable discharges from the Rangers. He urged his superior to publish in the pages of the *Galveston Daily News* an accurate account of how and why the company was disbanded.[38]

Major Jones remained unmoved by these pleas. He did not correct the false reports about the company's disbanding and the

Rangers' discharges, nor did he make a personal appearance in the riotous district on the Clear Fork as Campbell, Van Riper, and many aggrieved citizens had so strongly urged. He bowed instead to political pressures originating in the letters to the governor from Judge Fleming, Cornelius K. Stribling, and other influential Clear Fork figures, who had much to fear from a real investigation of recent local law-enforcement history. Word came down from the governor's office to Adjutant General Steele and thence to Jones: do nothing; let the county officials and local citizenry work out this problem.

It was a decision that would prove disastrous for John Larn. Soon Grangers, vigilantes, community leaders, and county law officers would arrive at a mutual agreement: the problems in Shackelford County could only be resolved by the elimination of the source of those problems, a man named John Larn and his confederates.

When it became clear that Major Jones was not coming to the troubled region, Campbell departed in disgust, leaving Sergeant Van Riper in command of the small Ranger force that remained at Camp Sibley. In his last letter to Jones, Campbell had mentioned the disappearance of Larn's nearest neighbor. That neighbor was A. J. Lancaster, an outspoken leader of the Grangers and Larn's bitter enemy. When he did not show up after several days his badly frightened wife sought out Sheriff Cruger, who organized a search. Deputy Sheriff Jim Draper found the missing man hiding in the brakes along the Clear Fork. Lancaster said Larn and Selman had chased him on horseback for miles, firing at him several times. Suffering a minor wound from one of the bullets, he had taken refuge in the brush along the river. He had successfully eluded his attackers, but had not gone home for fear of exposing his family to danger.[39]

Lancaster was a man of courage. It was Lancaster who, after watching Larn at his dirty work in February, had filed the first formal complaint against him, a complaint that led to the dragging of the river and the discovery of incriminating hides. In May he had promoted and signed the letter and petition to Major Jones that spelled out the depredations of Larn and his henchmen. Now he acted forthrightly again. Accompanied by William Brisky, another Granger and Larn neighbor, Lancaster went to Albany and told Justice of the Peace Edgar Rye he wanted to file charges against Larn and company.

From Sheriff Cruger, Rye had learned the details of Larn and Selman's latest outrage—the attempt on Lancaster's life. After Rye and Cruger consulted with other clan leaders, a decision was made that the time had come to deal decisively with John Larn. Victims were willing to swear out a complaint, and justification for an arrest was evident. Feeling against Larn was high among both the Grangers he had victimized and former friends and relatives who were tired of making excuses for a man they now saw as criminally brutal and a potential threat to their own safety. Due to the sharp reduction in Company B personnel, there was little chance Rangers would interfere in whatever plans the Tin Hats had for Larn after his arrest. Now was the time to act.

On June 21 Rye formalized the complaint of Lancaster and Brisky, charging that John M. Larn, John Selman, Thomas Curtis, John Gross, Thomas Selman, Jim Herrington, and one "Thistle" had at "diverse times . . . threatened to do some serious bodily hurt to the persons of deponents, and that deponents fear that [those accused] will carry their said threats into execution unless restrained therefrom by due course of law." Based on this complaint, sworn to and signed by both Lancaster and Brisky, Rye issued a warrant for the arrest of the seven men and turned it over to Sheriff Bill Cruger for execution.[40]

Rye issued the warrant on Friday, June 21. It took Cruger all of Saturday, the 22nd, to round up and deputize a posse large enough to take on the Larn-Selman combine. He rode around to the larger ranches, got the blessing of the patriarchs of the Reynolds and Matthews clans, and enlisted at least five young men who were related to Larn's wife by blood or marriage: John A. Matthews; Ben, George, and Glenn Reynolds; and Bill Howsley. Other possemen

John A. "Bud" Matthews, Larn's brother-in-law, was a member of the sheriff's posse that arrested him. Some said he also participated in Larn's execution.

included Deputy Sheriffs Dave Barker and John Poe, Fort Griffin Town Marshal Bill Gilson, and Jim Treadwell.[41]

The time Cruger took to assemble his posse enabled John and Tom Selman, Gross, and Herrington to escape. Word of the issuance of the warrants and Cruger's posse enlistment spread quickly throughout the area. When Hurricane Minnie at Fort Griffin heard the news, she saddled up and rode hard to warn her lover, John Selman.[42]

On Saturday night Sheriff Cruger divided his men into two groups to make the assault on the Larn and Selman ranch houses. The sheriff took a party of eight men to Larn's place. Another posse, which included Glenn Reynolds and Bill Howsley and was led by Cruger's chief deputy, Jim Draper, headed for Selman's Rock Ranch.

The possemen moved into positions around the houses during the night. In the morning the men at the Rock Ranch found only Selman's wife and children. The men they sought, warned by Hurricane Minnie, had flown.

Sheriff Cruger's posse had better luck. As dawn broke that Sunday morning, John Larn came out of the house with a bucket and, like any peaceful, bucolic farmer, walked unconcernedly to his cow pens to do the milking. Stealthily, with weapons at the ready, Cruger, Dave Barker, and Ben Reynolds approached Larn from behind and the sheriff announced in a loud voice that he had a warrant for his arrest.

There are several versions of Larn's reaction, all of them secondhand.

Edgar Rye, who must have heard the story of the arrest that day from Cruger, chose to recount a melodramatic exchange in his book. Larn, unarmed, watched the possemen approach with drawn six-shooters, and said:

> "Boys, it is the first time you ever caught me without my gun, or any chance to secure it. I'll give you $500 to allow my wife

to bring my gun to me, and I will take my chances with the whole bunch. Oh, I know, you are too big cowards to face me without the odds in your favor."

"All that reckless talk will do you no good now, Laren. We don't intend to sacrifice any lives to please your desire for a fight," replied Sheriff Cruger.[43]

Phin Reynolds remembered a different account as related by his brother Ben. In this version Larn was wearing a gun when Cruger, Barker, and Reynolds came up behind him. "Larn quietly unbuckled his belt and handed over his gun to Cruger," said Reynolds, but "when he saw that the warrant was from the court at Albany, he trembled and said that he would not have surrendered had he known that the warrant was from the Albany court."[44]

Newt Jones, one of the few Rangers still remaining at Camp Sibley, heard the story that same day from posse members. As he remembered it, Larn was armed, but calmly turned over his pistol to Cruger, remarking that he thought he had seen men around the house earlier, but thought they were Rangers.[45]

A newspaper account, published three weeks after the event, alleged that Larn asked Cruger to allow him to go back into the house, and when the request was denied, angrily declared that if he had been allowed to go he would have gotten a gun and killed them all. He then vowed that if he ever regained his freedom he would see every posse member dead. This last statement, according to the account, sealed his fate.[46]

Many details in these stories are implausible. It is not likely Larn would wear a sixshooter to milk the cows, but if he took a weapon out with him because he had seen men skulking about the place, he would hardly have been taken and disarmed so easily. If he had suspected at all that men were waiting for him outside, he surely would have sent his hired man, who was in the house, to do the milking.

He could not have been surprised that an arrest warrant presented by Shackelford County Sheriff Cruger had been issued by the court in Albany, the county seat. If he "trembled" and his demeanor suddenly changed, it was probably because Cruger told him he would not be taken to the military guardhouse at Fort Griffin that was often used by county officers, including Larn himself. There, Larn knew, army personnel with whom he had always been on good terms would protect him, and he would be safe from his enemies.

He may well have blanched at the thought of being locked up in the steamy, crowded, picket-house jail at Albany, where he would be shackled with the likes of Hurricane Bill and other common criminals, and at the mercy of those who would like to eliminate him. Quite possibly his composure was shaken when he recognized his wife's relatives among the posse. Their presence could only mean that he had lost the support and protection of the Matthews and Reynolds families. In that moment Larn's vaunted self-confidence may have shattered as he faced the stark reality that this could be the beginning of the end for him.

Larn is said to have called his wife and little boy from the house and, tightly holding young Will, now four and a half, told him to look closely at the men he saw there and remember them well. The implication is that Larn knew he was soon to die, that he also knew these men would participate in his execution, and he wanted his son to avenge his death when he grew to manhood.[47]

According to a version related by Frank Collinson, this scene took place later at the Albany jail. Larn's directive to his son was not implied, but quite clear: "These are my murderers," Larn is quoted. "They are going to kill me tonight. When you are big enough to use a gun, I want you to kill them all." Collinson said he heard this story from Hurricane Bill Martin, who was, of course, in the jail at the time.[48]

The story that Larn asked permission to return to the house to get a gun and fight the posse is ridiculous. The suggestion that he threatened retribution against the possemen and by so doing assured his own death is also difficult to swallow. John Larn had many faults, but stupidity was not one of them. Knowing the reaction such threats would certainly bring, he would not have voiced them unless he had already given up all hope of survival, and there is evidence that he had not.

He told Mary to bring Will and the hired man in a buggy and follow the posse. It has been suggested that he feared he might be lynched along the way and hoped his family's presence would prevent that.[49] This, too, is not likely, for Mary did not accompany the posse all the way to Albany. Acting on Larn's instructions, she took with her all the available cash from the house. When the posse reached Fort Griffin, she went in search of John W. Wray, a new arrival and about the only lawyer in the county who was not associated with the Tin Hat-Band Brigade, to enlist his aid in getting her husband freed.

Larn's captors put him on a horse with his hands tied and his legs secured by a rope under the animal. The party headed toward Fort Griffin, followed by Mary Jane, little Will, and the hired man in the buggy. As they rode out of Larn's yard, Deputy Sheriff Dave Barker leaned over to Ben Reynolds and, grinning, said, "We have got the nest egg," meaning the prize catch.[50]

From high ground some distance away John Selman watched the arrest of his friend and partner. After being alerted by Hurricane Minnie and escaping the Rock Ranch before Draper's posse arrived, the Selman brothers, John Gross, and Jim Herrington rode for Larn's place. Unfortunately for Larn, they found it already surrounded by other possemen and had to simply look on in silence as Larn was captured. Selman then led his followers southeastward out of Throckmorton and Shackelford into Stephens County.

On Sunday afternoon Sheriff Cruger and his posse brought their prisoner into Albany. The officers first took Larn to Charley Reinbold's blacksmith shop and had iron shackles placed on his legs. Shackelford County, still without a permanent jail, housed its prisoners in a windowless, twelve by fourteen feet picket building. It was located on Main Street south of the square, near the bridge crossing Hubbard Creek. There Larn, legs shackled, joined Hurricane Bill and eleven other prisoners.

Sheriff Cruger affirmed on the warrant for John Larn et al. that on June 23 he did arrest Larn, Thistle, and Thomas Curtis, but the others were not found in the county.[51] Ranger Sergeant Van Riper also reported that, in addition to Larn, Sheriff Cruger had apprehended Curtis and a man he called "Sissle" on that day.[52] Strangely, there seems to be no further mention of Thistle or Curtis in the records, reports, newspapers, or eyewitness accounts. The two men apparently vanished as the entire focus of interest centered on Larn. It appears that, with the "nest egg" in custody, no one cared to bother with prosecuting Thistle and Curtis. Newspapers did report, however, that a day or two later an unknown man was found hanging near Fort Griffin.[53] Perhaps vigilante justice had been meted out to at least one of the two.

After he delivered Larn to the Albany jail, Cruger rode all the way back to Treadwell's ranch in Throckmorton County, where an emergency meeting of the vigilantes had been called to determine the next move. Cruger sent a rider to the Ranger camp on Sibley Creek to ask Sergeant Van Riper and his few remaining Rangers to join them at Treadwell's. The message sounded urgent, according to Newt Jones, who remembered they were told to get to Treadwell's place "as soon as God would let us."[54]

All six of the Rangers—Sergeant Van Riper, Cpl. C. M. Sterling, and privates J. E. Hines, Jim McIntire, Jack Smith, and Newt Jones—rode over to Treadwell's where they found the Tin Hats in heated discussion about what to do with Larn. "The mob was there; all that bunch belonged, and now they were falling out among themselves," recalled Newt Jones. Cruger told Van Riper that the Selman brothers and John Gross had escaped to the southeast and he wanted the Rangers to pursue them. Van Riper, angry that his assistance had not been requested for the initial raids, refused. Newt Jones suspected the vigilance committee wanted the Rangers out of the way so they couldn't interfere with plans that were being made for Larn. Van Riper called his Rangers together and left in a huff. The committee meeting continued, and it is clear from what followed that a decision was reached: John Larn must die that night.

Edna Selman never doubted that outcome. Rangers Jones and Smith, who were acquainted with Old John's wife, stopped by the Rock Ranch to speak to her on their way back to Camp Sibley. "Mrs. Selman told us they would kill Larn that night," said Jones. "We were shocked. We hadn't thought they would go that far even though they were falling out among themselves."[55]

Meanwhile, it took Mary Jane Larn several hours to locate attorney John W. Wray in Fort Griffin and bring him to Albany. She obtained a room for herself and her son at George Shields's hotel while Wray hunted up Justice of the Peace Edgar Rye and tried desperately to get Larn released on bond. Rye refused, saying that bond release could not be granted without a hearing and it was too late in the day to hold a preliminary trial. In his book, *The Quirt and the Spur*, Rye quotes this exchange with the lawyer:

> "But, your Honor," said Wray, "we will place $1,200 in gold in your hands if you will give us the privilege of guarding him at the hotel over night."
>
> "Do you understand what that proposition means, Wray?"
>
> "It only means, your Honor, that we guarantee his presence in court to-morrow."
>
> "No, I am sorry to say, Wray, that your proposition spells bribery; and if it were not that the peculiar situation restrains me from giving forcible demonstration of my feelings, I would make it a personal matter with you."
>
> "But I beg your pardon, your Honor; I have good reasons to believe that my client's life is in danger from the Vigilance Committee, and I want to make every effort to protect him."
>
> "On the contrary, Wray, I have the best of reasons to believe that Sillman's *[sic]* gang will try to rescue Laren *[sic]*, and

I do not propose to interfere with Sheriff Cruger's arrangements to hold the prisoner. I understand that he already doubled the guards, and holds ten men in reserve."

"Well, your Honor, if Laren is killed during the night, I will not be responsible for it; I have tried to do my duty."

"No one can censure you for being true to your client, Wray. And I am also conscious of performing my duty as a State officer."[56]

Rye added that a vigilante eavesdropper heard this conversation and reported it back to the committee, but if, as was commonly believed, Rye himself was a member of the Tin Hats, that was unnecessary.

Whether Edgar Rye was involved in the conspiracy to assassinate John Larn is one of the mysteries of the Larn story. Wray's argument, as reported by Rye himself, was plausible; everyone in town knew that Larn, chained up in the jail, was at great risk of lynching. Rye's contention that Cruger had to keep him there to prevent a rescue by Selman is less convincing; surely Cruger could have amassed enough manpower to guard the prisoner in the Shields Hotel and turn back a rescue attempt.

The picket-house jail at Albany was a crude affair, but, as county officer Henry Herron proudly attested, no inmate ever escaped from its confines. The prisoners, all shackled with leg irons, were allowed to shuffle around the little building during the day, but at night were forced to lie down on rude pallets. A chain was then run between their legs above the shackles and fastened to opposite ends of the building. There were never less than two guards on duty.[57]

This routine was followed on the night of Sunday, June 23. As Rye had said, Sheriff Cruger had doubled the guard. Four deputies were there: Robert A. Slack, Henry Cruger, the sheriff's brother, former buffalo hunter John W. Poe, and saloonkeeper Edward E. Merritt. Slack would later claim that during the evening Larn called him to one side and offered him $1,500 if he would let him escape before midnight. He was sure, Larn said, that some time after that hour a mob would come to lynch him. Slack said he refused the bribe.[58]

Apparently it was common knowledge that John Larn was doomed, that the vigilantes would not permit him to see the light of another day. Edna Selman knew it. Attorney Wray knew it. Even John Larn knew it. Yet, if we are to believe the later sworn testimony of the jailers, the possibility of a lynch-mob raid on the jail concerned them little.

Slack and Merritt said they crawled into the guards' beds about ten o'clock and went to sleep, leaving Henry Cruger and John Poe on guard. Some time after midnight,[59] the neighborhood dogs started barking. Poe, who was sitting on a chair just inside the doorway, stood up and stepped to the door. "The first I knew," he said, "the dogs barked and I heard a noise like the tramping of men's feet. I looked around and saw a crowd of men. All I saw were armed. I raised up and halted them—drew my sixshooter. They pulled me out of the door and took my sixshooter away from me."

The intruders also quickly disarmed Henry Cruger. They wore slickers and the lower portions of their faces were covered with bandanas. Cruger estimated they numbered "about thirty to thirty-five;" Poe thought perhaps there were twenty in all. Some of them shouldered their way into the room and roused Slack and Merritt.

"When they woke me up," Merritt said, "two or three of them had their six shooters pulled down on me. I got mine out from under my head and they made me lay [it] down again."

Slack said he was awakened by "all the fuss in the house. There was four men stood over me with their six shooters cocked and told me to give up my pistol. . . . After them telling me two or three times, I raised up my pillow and they took the pistol."

The guards' testimony did not agree on the number of men who entered the building. Poe estimated ten or fifteen; Merritt said seven or eight; Slack saw five or six, but admitted there may have been more. After all four guards were disarmed the masked intruders

immediately turned their attention to John Larn. The chain lock-
down prevented them from taking their quarry out and suspend-
ing him from a tree as was their usual practice. Larn's execution
would have to be done by firing squad.

Merritt said they "strung across the room" facing Larn, who
spoke not a word. Four began shooting. Merritt estimated twenty
shots were fired.

Slack agreed that four men did all the shooting and he thought
they emptied their pistols.[60] "He was the gamest man I ever saw,"
Slack said later. "He placidly smiled on the mob as they shot him
to pieces."[61]

At the inquest Slack testified that after the burst of gunfire someone outside yelled, "That's enough," and then the gunmen left.

John Poe and Henry Cruger, standing outside, did not see the
actual shooting. Poe said he "heard a shot fired and then a short interval and then 10 or 20 shots fired in quick succession." Cruger
merely said, "I heard them shooting and John Larn was shot
dead."[62]

Their mission accomplished, the execution party left quietly,
walking south into the darkness.

It has been said that when she heard the gunfire Mary Larn ran
screaming from the Shields Hotel to the jail. The guards were carrying the blanket-wrapped body of her husband out when she
arrived.[63]

At an inquest held before Edgar Rye the next morning, the
guards told their stories and swore they were unable to recognize
any of the masked mob members. Not one of the primary witnesses
to the shooting—every single prisoner inside the jail—was called
to testify. Although Hurricane Bill Martin or other prisoners might
have been able to identify some of the gunmen, there was evidently no desire on the part of Rye or anyone else to have that happen.

The dozen prisoners in that picket house jail were indisputably
frozen in fear when the mob appeared. Chained to one another
and to the building, completely helpless, knowing that Larn was to

be killed but not knowing how many others the vigilantes might also shoot, accidentally or intentionally, they must have crawled as far from Larn as they could.

Hurricane Bill in particular, who had repeatedly bragged he could name all the vigilantes and recite their crimes, would have been terrified. Jailer Slack later told his family that Martin remarked coolly when he heard the mob approaching: "It would be a pity for them to bloody up my nice pallet, so I'll just get up," but that story is hardly believable. Slack called Martin "one of the wildest men we ever had in the West,"[64] and he may have been, but in the early hours of June 24, 1878, he had to be one of the luckiest men in the West. Not only did the vigilantes pass up the opportunity to kill him and close his mouth forever, but they arranged with Justice of the Peace Edgar Rye for his release from that bloodspattered jail. Martin had been held there almost three months awaiting trial on the assault to murder charge, but suddenly, with John Larn dead, it was decided he could be freed on his own recognizance. It was also suggested that he make himself scarce in Shackelford County, a suggestion with which he quickly complied.

Only hours after his release, Martin rode into Frank Collinson's buffalo camp on a badly jaded horse and told the story of the vigilante mob and Larn's execution. Collinson remembered that "Hurricane Bill trembled as he talked, so great was his fear of the Vigilantes and so narrow had been his escape. . . . 'I was scared to death,' he said. 'I thought I would be next, but they did not notice me, and later let me go when I promised to leave the country.' "[65]

After hearing the testimony of the guards, a coroner's jury—composed of hotelman J. Henry Barre, farmer Henry Palm, blacksmith Charley Reinbold, A. H. Miller, and E. H. Manning—found that the deceased, John M. Larn, had met his death as a result of "nine pistol shots through the body," and that "said shots were fired by unknown parties."[66]

These "unknown parties" have never been positively identified as residents of the region have been tight-lipped about the matter since 1878. It is almost certain that some of Larn's in-laws were among his executioners. Many years later Phin Reynolds recounted a conversation with Bill Howsley, who had married a cousin of Mary Jane Larn, in which Howsley told him there were nine men in the bunch that killed Larn and that he was one of them. Howsley would not identify any others, but did mention that the leader was a tall man. Reynolds remarked that the description fit Tom Merrill, a cowboy with the Horse Shoe outfit on the Double Mountain Fork who was believed to be a Tin Hat. Howsley then told him the leader was not Merrill, and hinted that he was one of Reynolds's own brothers.[67]

John Meadows was convinced that at least two of Larn's brothers-in-law participated in the execution. "Bud Matthews was in it to a dead moral certainty," he said in a 1935 interview. "There ain't no question in my mind about that. And so was Mart Hoover, another brother-in-law of Larn's."[68]

Hurricane Bill, who watched the shooting in horror, said that Sheriff Cruger was one of the execution party, and that "a close relative" of Larn gave him "the mercy shot," placing the muzzle of his pistol close to Larn's head and firing "to make sure he was dead."[69]

According to an account of the lynching published in the *Fort Worth Daily Democrat*, "Larn raised up on his couch and was recognized by one of the mob, who beckoned to some one nearer the door, when a member of the mob approached and shot Larn in the forehead, after which about twenty shots were fired into his body."[70] This would seem to provide some credence to Martin's story, although the "mercy shot" in this version was fired before, not after, the fusillade. It also agrees with John Poe's testimony that he heard a single shot and then, after an interval, from ten to twenty more in quick succession.

Word of Larn's bloody demise spread quickly throughout the Clear Fork country and created an uproar. On Monday, June 24, Texas Ranger Jim McIntire wired Major Jones from Fort Griffin:

Texas Ranger Jim McIntire wired the news of Larn's lynching to Major Jones in Austin. Courtesy of the Western History Collection, University of Oklahoma Library.

"John Lauren was arrested yesterday by sheriff posse and shot last night by mob while in jail. Your assistance is greatly needed as the Country is in terrible excitement."[71]

A few days later in his monthly report, Sergeant Van Riper said that "an organized vigilance committee [of] upwards of one hundred and fifty persons are in arms and scouting through the country, purchasing all the fire arms that is to be had. . . . On the night of the 24th a party of them numbering near one hundred, headed by Sheriff Cruger, were in Fort Griffin arming themselves."[72]

No one was more excited than Big Bill Gilson, town marshal of Fort Griffin. Gilson had been a staunch supporter of Larn and Selman, and now with Larn dead and Selman flown, he was afraid he would be the next target. He suddenly turned up missing. The *Jacksboro Frontier Echo* reported his disappearance, adding, "It is rumored that Big Bill knew considerable about the doings of the 'Tin Hat-Band Brigade' and some of the members were afraid Bill had or would blow on them."[73]

Ranger Jim McIntire later told a wild story of how Gilson, a hard drinker, got the "jim-jams" and showed up at Camp Sibley pleading for help in escaping the area. McIntire said he got Gilson a new set of clothes, took him down to the river, and had him change clothers. He then shot Gilson's old clothes full of holes and scattered them along the bank to give the impression that Gilson had been murdered and his body thrown in the Clear Fork. He said he put Gilson on a "big State mule" and rode with him all night to a hideout near Fort Belknap. Later he and other Rangers took the ex-marshal to Austin, where Gilson told the state officials all he knew about the Shackelford County vigilantes.[74]

The truth is often stretched in McIntire's accounts. He went on to say that as a result of Gilson's revelations, warrants were issued for "the whole outfit" of vigilantes and served by the Rangers. "They furnished bail and went down to 'square it' with the authorities. It cost them about $50,000 to get out of the scrape, and that broke up the vigilance business at Fort Griffin."[75]

This story reeks of exaggeration; no vigilantes were arrested. But Sergeant Van Riper did confirm in his June report to Major Jones that "W. C. Gilson, a member of the committee, publicly pronounced against them in the streets of Ft. Griffin to the immediate danger of his life. He was induced to leave town to save his life and render services to the state by giving his evidence against parties concerned in the committee."[76]

Newt Jones was sure the lives of the Rangers were in grave danger from the vigilantes when they began to investigate the lynching. When Jones met John Poe in Fort Griffin and announced that the Rangers were investigating Larn's death, he was prepared for trouble, for he knew Poe to be one of the Tin Hats. "I had my Winchester ready and my trigger finger in place," he recalled. Poe said not a word, but gave the Ranger a look that he remembered sixty-nine years later.

Still Jones did not let the matter rest. He saw his good friend Glenn Reynolds with a group of vigilantes and called him aside. He asked if the rumor was true—that if the Rangers continued to probe, they would receive the same treatment as Larn. "If you are going to get evidence," Reynolds answered, "there is nothing they will not do to stop you." Jones said a man approached Ranger Jack Smith and himself with a bribe to drop the investigation. "He told us we would get plenty of money, but Smith started cursing him and told him we did not want that kind of money and did not let him get any further."[77]

During the great excitement that gripped Shackelford County after the lynching, Gilson's defection and disappearance was of less concern to Sheriff Cruger and the aroused citizenry than the whereabouts of John Selman. Many feared Selman would return to have his revenge with a campaign of ambush and assassination. Cruger met with Van Riper again and the Ranger sergeant agreed to accompany a posse in the search for Selman.

After Hurricane Minnie warned him of his impending arrest, Old John and his followers had ridden downriver into Stephens

County, where they allowed themselves to be seen at the Tom Lanier ranch on Sunday, June 23. This was apparently an attempt to throw off any pursuing posse, for that night they doubled back to the Larn place. They found no one there, of course. Mary Jane, her son, and the hired man were in Albany where John Larn was about to be shot full of holes. A last-minute rescue of his partner, so feared by many, was not on Selman's mind. He was after Larn's prize stud horse, a $300 stallion named "Old Bab."

Astride this powerful mount, Selman led his followers west. On Monday, June 24, they stopped briefly at the Horse Shoe T Cross Ranch, Tom Merrill's outfit on the Double Mountain Fork of the Brazos, and then continued on. Cruger and Van Riper had picked up the trail and the following day arrived at the ranch. Then it was that foreman Tom Peeler and his hands first learned of Larn's death and that the Selman bunch were fugitives. One of Peeler's cowboys was John Meadows, who still harbored a deep hatred for both Larn and Selman. Meadows was happy to hear of Larn's death but was less pleased by Selman's escape. He told Peeler he was only sorry he had not been there when the original arrest warrants were issued. "Selman wouldn't have got away," he declared, "for I meant to kill that son-of-a-bitch." Now he asked permission to join the posse. "I'll trail him to hell," Meadows vowed. Peeler told him to take his best horse and wished him luck.[78]

Meadows caught up with the posse at Timber Creek on the south side of the Brazos. "I had the pleasure of trailing [Selman's party] for a hundred miles. . . . We stayed on the trail as long as we could," Meadows said. At a buffalo hunter's camp near Spring Lake, they found that the fugitives had exchanged their horses for fresh mounts. The posse had to abandon the chase. "Our horses was give out," said Meadows, sadly. They did find Larn's stallion, Old Bab, at the camp, however. Posseman Luke McCabe took charge of the valuable horse and returned him to Mary Jane Larn.[79]

Cruger did not get back to Fort Griffin until Sunday, June 30. He immediately sent a telegram to Major Jones in Austin: "Have

been absent—Just returned—Cannot bring Selman here alive—
Charges against him cannot be sustained in law—Nine chances to
one that the mob will hang him—Will you have him brought here
or shall I go for him—Answer."[80]

There is no record of an answer from Jones. John Larn was
dead; John Selman had fled the Clear Fork country and probably
the state. Hoping the mess in Shackelford County was over, Jones
believed that the adage about letting sleeping dogs lie applied to
missing and dead ones as well.

However, he changed his mind within two weeks and decided
that conditions on the Clear Fork were still volatile and required
the presence of the Texas Rangers. On July 13 he ordered Lt. G. W.
Arrington, commander of Company C in Erath and Comanche
Counties, to proceed to the area and establish a camp near Fort
Griffin. "On your arrival," he directed,

> you will immediately place yourself in communication with
> the civil officers of the county to aid them in executing pro-
> cess from the courts and in maintaining law and order, and in
> giving protection to the lives and property of all citizens. You
> will communicate also with reliable citizens to get informa-
> tion in regard to the troubles there.

The "reliable citizens" listed were for the most part members of
the vigilance committee or supporters of its actions—specifically
the elimination of Larn and Selman.[81]

Lieutenant Arrington arrived in the area on July 31 and set up
camp on Lambshead Creek, five miles northwest of Fort Griffin.
He reported finding everything quiet, but was aware of "a very
strong feeling against the old Co. of Rangers." He said it was evident that in that section Rangers were "below par with all classes."[82]
After he "conversed with quite a number of the good citizens" over
the next few weeks, Arrington concluded "that at one time nearly

everybody belonged to the mob," but those citizens now believed law and order could be maintained without recourse to lynch law.[83]

Their view proved correct. After the terrible events of June 1878, the Tin Hat-Band Brigade no longer played a role in the lives of Shackelford County citizens. Horse theft, cattle rustling, and gunplay were not eliminated, of course, but after Larn's death the settlers left the criminals to the duly constituted law-enforcement officials.

It is a final irony that John Larn, one of the original leaders of the Tin Hats, was the organization's last victim.

Afterword

*"Larn's demise at the hands of the vigilantes [was] a sordid af-
fair which, in this writer's opinion, should have taken place long
before it occurred."*

J. R. WEBB

Mary Jane Larn took the bullet-riddled body of her
husband, dead at the age of twenty-nine, back to the home they
had shared for only three years, and buried it beside the grave of
their first child. Later a fine stone monument was erected over the
grave with a simple inscription.

JOHN M. LARN
BORN
MAR. 1, 1849,
DIED
JUNE 24, 1878.[1]

There is no question that Mary Jane was deeply in love with John Larn and was emotionally shattered by his brutal death. Famed cowboy author and Pinkerton detective Charlie Siringo claimed he saw her two years afterward and that she was still distraught. "At the mention of Johnny Larn's name she would cry like a baby," he said.[2]

Shackelford County historian J. R. Webb, who was acquainted with her in later years, said she "never knew to the day of her death the members of the mob, although she sensed the members and from whose ranks they were taken. She was one of the saddest looking women I have ever known and the grief always showing in every line of her face I shall always remember."[3]

For two years Mary Jane mourned her dead husband. Then, on October 23, 1880, she married a Presbyterian minister, the Reverend John Brown. He moved into the Larn ranch house with Mary Jane and Will. Within a week of the marriage, the Reverend Brown sold Larn's cattle and invested the money in a flock of sheep.[4] If confirmed cattleman John Larn stirred angrily in his grave over this move, he must have flipped over completely when that same year Brown had Will's name legally changed from Larn to Brown.[5]

The Clear Fork was not sheep country, but Brown stubbornly continued his attempt to raise sheep there until finally giving up in 1886. In June of that year he turned the ranch over to his brother-in-law John A. Matthews on a four-year lease arrangement. The Browns moved to Albany, where Reverend Brown preached. In 1887 Brown was instrumental in bringing the celebrated "Angel of the Battlefield," Clara Barton, then president of the American Red Cross, to Albany for a tour of the miserable local conditons brought on by the severe drought of that year.[6]

Three children were born to the Reverend Brown and the former Mary Jane Larn.[7] About 1887 Brown moved his family to Fall River, Massachusetts. Will did not go with them, but remained in Texas, living in the home of his grandfather, Joseph B. Matthews.

A photograph of John Larn's grave, taken in the year 2000. Note the coins someone has placed on the base. Courtesy of Julia Putnam.

In February 1890 Joe Matthews applied for and was granted legal guardianship of his sixteen-year-old grandson, then known as Willie A. Brown. The boy, Matthews affirmed, was heir to his father's estate, valued at $10,000.[8] Several months later Matthews filed suit against Brown on behalf of his grandson, claiming Will was entitled to half of the proceeds of the Larn stock sold in 1880, with interest.[9] He got a favorable judgment, but Brown, still in Massachusetts, refused to make payment. The matter was resolved in September 1891 when John and Mary Jane Brown turned over the old Larn property to Joe Matthews, who then deeded it to Will.[10]

Mary Jane, in far-off Massachusetts, was not happy. She left Brown and, with their three children, returned to Texas. A divorce followed in 1895.

In 1896 Brown published a strange book entitled *Twenty-Five Years a Parson in the Wild West,* purportedly based on the life of one Parson Ralph Riley, but actually a thinly disguised semi-fictional autobiography. One chapter, "The Unlucky Ranch," dealt with the Larn house and property, which Brown considered cursed. He told of the brutal death of the original owner, unnamed, but obviously John Larn, the lack of success at cattle and sheep raising by the widow and her new clerical husband, and the failure of later owners, including a watermelon farmer. "Others also rented or bought the place," wrote Brown, "but the same bad luck followed all alike, and the man who now owns it has not procured it justly, and when he is through with it he is likely to say that his ranch was a bag with holes in the bottom."[11] He was referring, presumably, to his stepson Will, then twenty-two years old, who was in control of the property at the time.

Brown's book implies that John Larn's difficulties on the Clear Fork all derived from bad relations with Mary's family, beginning immediately after the marriage. As Brown told it, Mary's brother, Bud Matthews, resented the dowry of five hundred fine young cows his father presented to Larn, and drove the herd off, replacing it with a bunch of "old scrubs." When Larn learned what his brother-

Reverend John Brown married Larn's widow. Courtesy of Julia Putnam.

in-law had done, he "sent him his old cows and told him to go to Jericho with them or somewhere else not so far away. This led to family feuds and bad blood in the neighborhood generally."[12] In another chapter Brown writes bitterly of his marriage to Mary Jane Larn: "The conjugal voyage . . . lasted just fifteen years and then the bark was beached. . . . Oh, it is a thousand times better to be disappointed in courtship than deceived in marriage."[13]

Soon after the book was published, John Brown died.[14] Mary Jane has been quoted as remarking of her two husbands: "I married a cow thief the first time, and a preacher the second, and I do believe the cow thief was the best man."[15] Mary Jane Matthews Larn Brown lived out her final years in California. According to historian C. L. Sonnichsen, "through all the years she blamed some of her closest relatives for what happened [to Larn] and she never once admitted that [he] deserved what he got."[16] In 1930 a story about Larn published in the *Albany News* incensed his widow. She wrote to John A. Matthews, her brother, and accused him of planting the article and defaming the memory of John Larn. Matthews, "keenly hurt" by her attitude, told his grandson that the Larn story was "part of the history of this area," and he could not have prevented its publication had he wanted. Rumors that he had participated in Larn's execution were untrue, he said, but he made it clear "he thought Larn deserved to be killed." So assiduously had the Matthews clan avoided mention of John Larn within the family that Joseph Blanton, the grandson of John A. and Sallie Matthews, had never heard Larn's story until its publication in the *Albany News* and the arrival of Mary Jane's vitriolic letter.[17]

As late as 1946 Mary Jane wrote to Albany asking that Larn's grave be attended to.[18] She died on February 12 of that year in Los Angeles and was buried in Forest Lawn Cemetery in Glendale, California.[19]

In 1898 Will Larn, whose legal name then was Willie A. Brown, sold the old Larn ranch to his uncle, John A. Matthews, for $5,124. A year later he legally changed his name back to William A. Larn.[20]

William Larn, the only son of John and Mary Jane who survived childhood, led a stormy life before his death in Arizona. He is buried in Glendale, California. Photo by Jim Browning, courtesy of Janice McCravy.

Although he did not grow up to gun down his father's slayers, Will's later life was not devoid of violence. He worked cattle like his father, and, like his father, got into serious scrapes. In a fight at the Cowboys' Reunion at Haskell, Texas, in 1898, he was stabbed and nearly killed.[21] On October 1, 1907, at the age of thirty-three, he secretly enlisted in the Arizona Rangers to work as an undercover operative assigned to breaking up a gang of cattle rustlers in the northern part of the territory. "We expect great things from this man Larn," exulted Ranger Capt. Harry Wheeler. "No one at all knows that he is a Ranger."[22] Great things did not come to pass, however. Will Larn resigned on December 31, 1907, after serving only three months. Much disappointed by Larn's performance, Wheeler wrote "service unsatisfactory" on his personnel file, and, in a letter to the governor, remarked that the man was "not deserving of a good discharge."[23]

Following his short stint in the Arizona Rangers, Will Larn worked as a cowboy on the Reynolds brothers' ranch in Culberson and Jeff Davis Counties in Texas.[24] He developed locomotor ataxia at an early age, became a wheelchair invalid and, according to J. R. Webb, "became a charge upon the Matthews and Reynolds families."[25] Never having married, he spent his last years alone in Douglas, Arizona, where he died on June 3, 1937. He was buried at Glendale, California.[26]

After buying the old Larn house and ranch from Will in 1898, John A. Matthews kept the property for eight years. Some say it was Bud who removed the distinctive cupola from the roof of the house, and that his wife, Sallie, refused to live there because of the John Larn association.[27] Whatever the reason, Matthews sold a parcel of land totaling almost 2,200 acres to Joseph Barnett Putnam in 1906. The property sold included the Larn house and the old Honeymoon Cottage. The Putnam family has maintained residence and operated the ranch ever since.[28]

Fort Griffin, both the military post and the wild town of the same name, died not long after John Larn. As the violent decade of the 1870s came to an end, so did the threat of Indian raids and the need for the fort. At sundown on May 31, 1881, the flag at Fort Griffin was lowered for the last time. The few remaining troops left, abandoning the military installation.[29]

By this time the vast buffalo herds had disappeared from the Texas plains, and disappearing also were the hunters, dealers, and buyers who had traded in hides and made The Flat their head-quarters. The steel of new railroads stretched across Texas spelling the end of the great cattle drives to the railheads of Kansas, and rambunctious drovers no longer whooped and hollered in the streets of Fort Griffin. Editor G. W. Robson moved his newspaper, the *Echo*, from Jacksboro to Fort Griffin in January 1879, just in time

The Larn ranch house in 1913, a few years after it was acquired by the Putnam family. Courtesy of Julia Putnam.

The Larn ranch house in 1999, still the residence of the Putnam family.

to chronicle the decline of the fort and the town. Only three years later, in January 1882, he was forced to close his Fort Griffin operation and move to Albany. He entitled his last Fort Griffin editorial "Finis."[30]

With the soldiers, buffalo hunters, and cattle drovers gone, businesses moved out and the town of Fort Griffin slowly died. A century later, the flood plain below Government Hill, once the location of the wildest, toughest town in Texas, is only a quiet field.

Lieutenant Arrington and Company C of the Texas Rangers departed the Clear Fork in September 1879. No other company was assigned to replace them. This was a sure sign that the outlawry, vigilantism, and feuding that had plagued the area for years had greatly diminished, if not entirely disappeared.

Some of the characters who played significant roles in the John Larn drama went on to successful later careers.

John A. "Bud" Matthews, twenty-seven at the time of the Larn lynching, had married Sallie Ann Reynolds on Christmas Day in 1876. They had nine children, including Watt Reynolds Matthews, who would maintain the family ranch tradition until his death in 1997 at the age of 98. In the years following the Larn tragedy, John A. Matthews consolidated and expanded his cattle-raising operation as the J. A. Matthews Ranch Company, headquartered at Lambshead Ranch. He served as Shackelford County judge in 1895 and '96, and, in collaboration with members of the Reynolds family, in 1898 established Reynolds Presbyterian Academy, later known as Reynolds Presbyterian College, at Albany. In 1936 Sallie Ann published her notable history of the Reynolds and Matthews families, *Interwoven: A Pioneer Chronicle*. She died in 1938 and her husband three years later. They were buried in Albany.[31]

George, Bill, Ben, and Phin Reynolds did well in the cattle business and eventually established ranches in New Mexico, Arizona, Montana, and North Dakota as well as in many counties of Texas. In 1883 George and William, in association with former district judge J. R. Fleming, one-time Griffin storekeeper Frank Conrad, and others, organized the First National Bank of Albany. George Reynolds served as president of the bank from 1884 until 1905. He also helped organize the First National Bank in Oklahoma City.[32]

Another Clear Fork veteran who became a banker was John W. Poe, one-time member of the Tin Hat-Band Brigade and a guard at the Albany lock-up the night John Larn was executed. After Bill Gilson's sudden disappearance, Poe, then twenty-six years of age, accepted an appointment as town marshal of Fort Griffin. He held the post for a year, but in 1879 transferred to Mobeetie, Texas, another tough army town outside Fort Elliott in Wheeler County. There he worked as a stock detective for the Canadian River Cattle Association. He went to Lincoln, New Mexico, in 1881, became a deputy under Sheriff Pat Garrett, and helped track down and kill the notorious "Billy the Kid" Bonney. Lincoln County voters elected Poe sheriff in 1882, and he served two terms with distinction. In 1883 he married Sophie Alberding, a California girl who would later glorify her husband in an obsequious memoir entitled *Buckboard Days*. After resigning as sheriff at the end of 1885, Poe devoted his attention to ranching, the mercantile business, and banking. From 1893 to 1899 he served as president of the Bank of Roswell, which, when it opened in 1890, was the only institution of its kind within 225 miles. In 1900 he organized the Citizens' Bank of Roswell with himself as president. His enterprises prospered and Poe became a wealthy man. He died at Roswell, New Mexico, in 1923.[33]

John Shanssey, the former prizefighter who kept the Bee Hive Saloon and Dance Hall where Billy Bland and Charley Reed instigated one of The Flat's deadliest gunfights, left Fort Griffin in late 1878 and for the next twenty years operated a succession of saloons in Palo Pinto, Gordon, Abilene, Colorado City, and other Texas boom camps. By 1899 he had settled in Yuma, Arizona Territory, where he was elected mayor. He served several terms before leaving office in 1910. He became the Yuma County supervisor and still held that post when he died in a Los Angeles hospital in 1917.[34]

More striking than the list of Larn's contemporaries who achieved success is the remarkable number who, like Larn, died violently.

Charley Reed, Billy Bland's pal, after beating his hasty retreat from Fort Griffin after the bloody shootout of January 1877, led the life of a desperado for two more years. He was indicted for murder in April 1878 by the Shackelford County grand jury, but he continued to work for the Millett brothers, whose range harbored many fugitives from justice. Reed drove cattle up the trail to Dodge City in 1877 and '78. On September 14, 1878, officers arrested him in San Antonio, but, released on a writ of *habeas corpus,* he fled Texas and headed north to Nebraska. In May 1879 he shot and killed a man named Henry Loomis in a quarrel over a prostitute in Sidney, Nebraska. A mob with a rope marched him to a telegraph pole. Before dying, he is said to have admitted killing five men in Texas. A braggadocio to the end, Reed told his executioners that he "would jump and show them how a brave man died."[35]

The old assault to murder charge against another Fort Griffin desperado, Hurricane Bill Martin, was finally dismissed in February 1879. Drifting on, Martin was briefly the town marshal of Otero, New Mexico, a short-lived end-of-track town on the Sante Fe line. He added to his notoriety by joining the crowd of thieving gamblers and footpads who followed the track as it built through New Mexico. The date and manner of his death is in dispute. One Fort Griffin old-timer thought he died at Alamosa, Colorado,[36] but Frank Collinson remembered that he was killed a year or two later in the San Simon Valley of Arizona.[37] Another report placed his death at Calico, an obscure mining camp near Barstow, California.[38] There were newspaper stories that he killed himself.[39] Robert Millard, a pioneer settler of Rice County, Kansas, claimed Hurricane Bill died there as a result of an accidental gunshot wound.[40]

Cheap John Marks, the Fort Griffin merchant and realtor with whom Larn had negotiated property transactions, took up with

Hurricane Minnie after Martin and Selman so hurriedly departed The Flat. The *Fort Griffin Frontier Echo* of June 14, 1879, reported that "B. Marks (alias Cheap John) and Mrs. Minnie Martin" appeared on the police docket, charged with "living in adultry *[sic]*." About this time Marks sold his store in The Flat and left town. A Fort Worth gambler named Frank Schmidt shot and killed him on the prairie and returned to town wearing Cheap John's $18 boots. Schmidt explained he had collected a debt Marks had welshed on, and nothing more was said.[41]

When Throckmorton County was organized in March 1879, Glenn Reynolds was elected sheriff and served in that office until November 2, 1880.[42] Like John and Mary Jane Brown, he tried sheep raising in the early '80s, and, like the Browns, lost money in the venture. In February 1882 he reportedly shot and killed a man described as a "Mexican desperado" in an argument over a billiard game in a Fort Davis saloon.[43] In 1885 he moved to Arizona and returned to cattle ranching. The outbreak of the bloody Pleasant Valley War prompted him to migrate to Globe in Gila County, where he was elected sheriff in November 1888. A year later, on November 2, 1889, he was escorting the noted "Apache Kid" and other convicted Indian prisoners to the territorial prison at Yuma when his charges attacked and killed him.[44]

Big Bill Gilson stayed clear of Fort Griffin after Larn was lynched. In 1881 he took the town marshal's job at Sweetwater in Nolan County, Texas, where he was said to have added two more notches to the pistol handle of his sawed-off shotgun. In 1883 he was a hired gun in a fence-cutting war in Garza County, and the following year returned to Sweetwater. There he met his death at the hands of a tough gunman named Jim Cooksey.[45]

Bill Cruger—who rode with Larn during the Tin Hat raids, served as a deputy under him, incurred his enmity by killing Billy Bland, replaced him as sheriff, led the posse that arrested him, and may well have been a member of the execution squad that murdered him—served two more years as Shackelford County sheriff.

When he resigned on July 29, 1880, Editor G. W. Robson praised him in the *Fort Griffin Frontier Echo* as "the finest sheriff in the State, . . . a gallant, brave and efficient officer [who] has never faltered in the least, even at the very muzzle of the six-shooter."[46] The county commissioners followed up on the *Echo*'s praises by passing a series of resolutions honoring Cruger for "his efficiency and ability as a faithful, prompt, punctual and fearless officer."[47]

Cruger and his family returned to his native Georgia, but then he took the position as city marshal at Princeton, Kentucky. On December 29, 1882, he arrested City Attorney Charles F. Wing for drunkenness and disorderly conduct, but failed to search him thoroughly. As he escorted Wing to the police station, the man suddenly produced a pistol, whirled, and shot the officer just above the right eye. Bill Cruger, thirty-four, died within minutes.[48]

Cruger's chief deputy, Jim Draper, had also figured prominently in the arrest of Larn and the hunt for Selman. Many believed he, too, was one of Larn's executioners. Draper, a regular at the Fort Griffin dives, consorted with the sporting crowd even after marrying a girl named Frances Cooper in December 1878 and fathering several children. He paid gambling fines and often got into scrapes, including one with Robert A. Jeffress, who was one of the casualties in the Billy Bland gunfight of '77, and another with a man named Ed Russell, who stabbed Draper three times. Draper survived these altercations and later moved to Colorado. At the age of thirty-five he was killed at Raton, New Mexico, in 1889.[49]

Dave Barker, the Cruger deputy who remarked when Larn was arrested that they had "got the nest egg," was a native of Missouri, twenty-six years old in 1878. Four years earlier he had married fifteen-year-old Lottie Durkin, a former Indian captive, and the couple had several children. Barker continued on as deputy sheriff until December 1881 when he resigned, declaring, according to a newspaper report, that the position was "calculated to produce the complaint known as vexation of spirit and [was] hard work for poor pay." He ran a meat market in Fort Griffin for a time, but about

1883 moved with Lottie and the children to Mobeetie in the Texas panhandle. There he served as constable and coroner. Late in 1886 the Barkers moved to Tascosa in Oldham County where Dave again pinned on a badge. Lottie died the following year. Barker next appeared in Catskill, New Mexico Territory, where he opened another butcher shop. There, in November 1890 he quarreled with James T. Gibbons, claiming the Gibbons dog had bitten one of his children. Barker took a rifle and killed the dog; Gibbons took a sixshooter and killed Barker.[50]

Tom Merrill was another man thought to be a member of the Tin Hat-Band Brigade and to have participated in the elimination of John Larn.[51] Merrill, who cowboyed for the Horse Shoe outfit, was a tall, slim fellow, which fit the description of one of the men on Larn's firing squad. It was said he harbored a particular hatred for John Selman, who once tried to cheat him in a poker game. Some time after Larn's death, Merrill and his young wife left the Clear Fork country for new range, settling on the Rio Grande near Sierra Blanca in west Texas. In May 1885 someone ransacked their house and brutally murdered them both. Merrill was disemboweled and his head severed. His wife died from multiple stab wounds. Some suspected smugglers or disgruntled Mexican employees of the barbaric double murder, but no one was ever charged.[52]

At least one veteran of old Fort Griffin thought he knew who was responsible for the Merrill murders. In his memoirs, buffalo hunter Skelton Glenn stated flatly that Old John Selman hired two Mexicans to murder the Merrills. Selman's motive, Glenn believed, was his long-held enmity from the gambling clash of years before.[53] But if a vengeance-driven Selman did in fact contract the Merrill murders, it is more likely that he acted in retaliation for Merrill's role in the execution of John Larn.

Selman, like Larn and so many others, was destined to meet a violent end, but many years passed before Death caught up with wily Old John. During those years his life would be an almost unparalleled record of villainy.

His first crime after fleeing Sheriff Cruger's posse in June 1878 was committed in the Llauo Estacado, where he and his remaining followers—his brother Tom Cat and John Gross—encountered a party led by Texas horse dealer Fred Tucker. With seven wagons and twelve men as herders, Tucker was driving a herd of horses to market at Leadville, Colorado. The Selmans and Gross were welcomed into the Tucker camp, but repaid the hospitality during the night by grabbing all the available firearms, looting the wagons, and stealing the best of the horses.[54]

Charlie Siringo said that about this time Selman rode into his camp on the Canadian River and lay over for two days to rest his tired mount and replenish his ammunition with Siringo's reloading equipment. According to Siringo, Selman continued on toward New Mexico and came across two young Mexican boys driving a flock of two thousand sheep. He killed the boys, stole the flock, and later sold the sheep for a dollar a head.[55]

Selman's biographer discounts this story as farfetched,[56] although it is at least partially confirmed in John Selman, Jr.'s sketch of his father's life.[57] But true or not, the fact that many who knew him believed Selman fully capable of atrocities like this and the horrible Merrill murders speaks volumes about the man. Siringo said Selman "would kill and steal through pure cussedness,"[58] and to John Meadows he was cold-blooded and heartless, a man with "no soul whatever."[59]

In New Mexico Selman headed for Seven Rivers, a notorious hangout for outlaws. Taking advantage of the chaos there during the Lincoln County War, he quickly assumed leadership of a large outlaw gang and began a campaign of terrorism seldom equaled in the American West. Selman's Scouts, as they were called, attacked villages, stealing, looting, and indiscriminately destroying property. They raped women and butchered unarmed men and boys. When New Mexico Governor Lew Wallace in March 1879 drew up a list of the most wanted desperadoes in the territory, Old John Selman's name appeared third and Tom Cat Selman's fourth.[60] Under one of the many aliases he used after fleeing Shackleford County, John Selman was indicted in Lincoln County for murder in April 1879, but never came to trial.

Thomas "Tom Cat" Selman seems finally to have left his brother during this murderous campaign in New Mexico. According to John Meadows, Tom left the gang at Rocky Arroyo, just south of Seven Rivers, and went back to his wife and two children. The last Meadows heard of Tom Cat, he was living in Oklahoma.[61]

When things got too hot in New Mexico, John Selman returned to Texas. The Tascosa area became his headquarters, and he attempted to organize all the roving outlaw bands in west Texas into a great horse- and cattle-stealing confederacy. He hoped to control outlawry from the panhandle to the Mexican border, but this ambitious undertaking collapsed when Selman came down with Mexican black smallpox at Fort Davis and almost died.[62]

Back in Shackelford County, warrants for Selman's arrest had been issued and circulated in the surrounding counties. A grand jury in October 1878 had indicted John on nine counts of cattle theft and his brother Tom on three. To an *alias capias* issued on May 20, 1879, Judge J. R. Fleming appended a physical description of Old John and a tip: "If a whore by the name of Hurricane Minnie is around, there will John Selman be."[63]

Selman stayed on at Fort Davis after his bout with smallpox and, using the name "Captain John Tyson," opened a butcher shop. This he used to dispose of cattle stolen by a local rustling gang led by the notorious Jessie Evans. When Texas Rangers broke up the gang after a spirited gun battle, they recognized "John Tyson" as John Selman, the fugitive from Shackelford County. On June 22, 1880, Ranger Sgt. L. B. Caruthers reported that he had Selman in custody and that the prisoner, like Hurricane Bill Martin two years earlier, had offered to identify the Shackelford County vigilantes in exchange for leniency in his own cases. Selman subsequently did name, among others, Judge W. H. Ledbetter, Bill Gilson, Jim Draper, John Poe, John Jacobs, and George Mathews.[64]

However, two years after the Larn lynching and Selman escape, Shackleford County had moved on. Life was much quieter and passions had cooled. Folks in Shackleford County were not anxious to have Old John back in their midst again, stirring up old enmities and embarrassing leading men of the community. Sheriff Cruger wrote Major Jones that it was unlikely charges against Selman would stand up in court, and "the indictments were probably found in order to keep him out of the country, as he is a great thief and scoundrel and withal so sharp that he cannot be caught in his rascality." Cruger said he would not accept responsibility for protecting Selman's life if he were returned. "I fear the arrival of Selman will be a renewal of the times we have passed through," he said.[65] The trepidation Cruger felt over Selman's imminent return may have precipitated his decision to resign as sheriff; within a month he was gone.

Despite Cruger's misgivings, the Rangers took Selman to Comanche, where he was held in jail awaiting the opening of court in Shackelford County. On September 9, 1880, Sheriff D. H. Cunningham of Comanche County arrived in Albany with Selman and turned him over to Shackelford County officers.[66]

Placed in the same lock-up where his pal John Larn had died in a roar of gunfire, Selman must have been extremely nervous, but he did not remain there long. His guards, Bill Jeffries, Bill Howsley, and George Shields, soon removed his chains and took him up the road to Fort Griffin, ostensibly "to see if he could raise bail." At The Flat, said Phin Reynolds,

> they took him back of Conrad's store and gave him a horse and saddle, shook hands with him and told him to go. The guards shot off their pistols as he escaped. Jeffries claimed at first that he stumbled and fired his gun by mistake, but they afterwards admitted, at least Jeffries did, that they fired to make out as if they were trying to stop him. Selman escaped on a flea-bitten horse belonging to John Sauers. As Sauers

was working for George Reynolds at the time, George gave him another horse.[67]

John Selman rode long and hard for the Mexican border, stopping in Fort Davis only long enough to pick up his new wife, a woman he had married two days before he was arrested. Edna, his first wife and the mother of his four children, had died suddenly a short time after his first flight from the Clear Fork, and the children had been taken in by one of her nieces.[68]

In Mexico Selman prospected and ran saloons and gambling operations. When the authorities in Shackelford County dropped the charges against him in April 1888, he ventured back across the border and settled in El Paso. There he held the office of constable and engaged in the sixshooter episodes for which he is best remembered.

On April 5, 1894, in a wild shootout in Tillie Howard's sporting house, he shot and killed Deputy U.S. Marshal Baz Outlaw after Outlaw had mortally wounded Texas Ranger Joe McKidrict and severely injured Selman. Then, on August 19, 1895, he achieved his greatest fame—or infamy—by shooting to death the most celebrated gunfighter and mankiller in the red-hued history of frontier Texas: John Wesley Hardin. All the evidence indicated that Selman stepped into El Paso's Acme Saloon while Hardin was standing at the bar, and, without a word, shot his victim in the back of the head. Selman claimed, however, that he only drew and fired after Hardin looked him in the eye and went for his gun. To explain this apparent impossibility, Selman's defense attorney, Albert Bacon Fall, later a central figure in the Teapot Dome scandal during the Harding administration, cleverly suggested that the gaze of the two gunmen had met in the mirror behind the bar, that Hardin had made a hostile move, and Selman had been quicker. The argument raised sufficient doubt in the minds of the jury members that they were unable to reach a verdict.

Before a second trial was held, Deputy U.S. Marshal George Scarborough abruptly ended the bloody career of John Selman. In

El Paso Constable John Selman shortly before his death at the hands of a fellow lawman in 1896. Courtesy of the Nita Stewart Haley Memorial Library, Midland, Tex.

the early hours of Easter Sunday, April 5, 1896, in an alley beside
El Paso's Wigwam Saloon, Scarborough put four bullets into Selman, who died in agony on the afternoon of April 6. Scarborough
stood trial for murder, claimed self-defense, and was acquitted.[69]
Old Selman-hater John Meadows grumbled, "George Scarborough
killed that old son-of-a-bitch at El Paso, but it was forty years too
late."[70]

Shackelford County historian J. R. Webb came to much the
same conclusion regarding Selman's long-time partner: "Larn's
demise at the hands of the vigilantes [was] a sordid affair which, in
this writer's opinion, should have taken place long before it occurred."[71]

It would be an exaggeration to say that John Selman was a monster created by John Larn; Selman was undoubtedly a vicious man
who would have had a brutal career had he never met Larn. But
each man seemed to bring out and magnify the worst qualities of
the other. Clear Fork old-timers were hard put to say which was
worse. John Meadows, who despised them both, thought "old John
Selman was the meanest of the two. He was the meanest man that
ever lived."[72]

But John A. "Bud" Matthews gave the nod to his brother-in-law:
"John Selman was a dangerous man, but compared to John Larn,
he was a gentleman. Larn was the meanest man I ever knew."[73]

It was obviously a very difficult choice to make.

Abbreviations

AGF Adjutant General's Files. Archives Division, Texas State Library and Archives, Austin.

CLS Dr. C. L. Sonnichsen Papers. University of Texas at El Paso.

EPL E. P. Lamborn Collection. Kansas State Historical Society, Topeka.

FCP Collinson, Frank. "Three Texas Trigger Men." Manuscript in Frank Collinson Papers, Historical Research Center, Panhandle-Plains Historical Museum, Canyon, Tex.

FSM Fort Sill, Okla., Guard Reports, Fort Sill Museum Archives.

HGC Comstock, Henry Grisold. "Some of My Experiences and Observations on the Southwestern Plains of 1871 and 1872." Old Jail Art Center and Archive, Albany, Tex.

JCI Irwin, John Chadourne. "Frontier Life of John Chadbourne Irwin." Edited by Hazel Best Overton. Manuscript in Historical Research Center, Panhandle-Plains Historical Museum, Canyon, Tex.

JDF   James H. Draper File. Old Jail Art Center and Archive, Albany Tex.

JEH   J. Evetts Haley Collection. Nita Stewart Haley Memorial Library, Midland, Tex.

JRS   Selman, John R., Jr. "John Selman of El Paso." Manuscript in Texas State Library, Austin

JRW   J. R. Webb papers. Rupert Richardson Research Center, Hardin-Simmons University Library, Abilene, Tex.

NA   Fort Griffin, Tex., Post Records and Correspondence, Record Group 393, National Archives, Washington, D.C.

RBM   Burns, Rollie. "Reminiscenses of 56 Years." Manuscript in Nita Stewart Haley Memorial Library, Midland, Tex.

RG   Record Group

TSA   Texas Ranger Frontier Battalion Records. Texas State Archives.

Notes

FOREWORD

1. Some have suggested that the character of John Gant as played by Audie Murphy in the 1959 Universal Picture film *No Name on the Bullet* was based on Larn, but I do not see it. Among other things, Gant was a pariah who lived on at the end of the film. Larn, however, passed for a pillar of the community but was ultimately killed by that community.

INTRODUCTION

1. C. F. Eckhart, letter to the author, January 14, 1999.
2. Charles Robinson III, letter to the author, June 17, 1992.
3. C. L. Sonnichsen, *I'll Die Before I'll Run*, 342.
4. J. R. Webb to Mary Southerland, March 8, 1947, JRW.
5. Leon Metz, *The Shooters*, 231.
6. Leon Metz, letter to the author, July 28, 1996.
7. Frances Mayhugh Holden, *Lambshead Before Interwoven*, 155.
8. *Galveston Daily News*, July 13, 1878.
9. Edgar Rye, *The Quirt and the Spur*, 106.
10. Ibid., 103.
11. Ibid., 114.

12. Don H. Biggers, *Shackelford County Sketches,* 66–67.

13. Quoted in Joseph Edwin Blanton, *John Larn,* 12.

14. Quoted in Holden, *Lambshead Before Interwoven,* 157.

15. Leon Metz, *John Selman,* 52–53.

16. Quoted in Holden, *Lambshead Before Interwoven,* 157.

17. As his wife inscribed his gravestone.

18. U.S. Census, Calhoun County, Ala., 1860.

19. J. R. Webb to Lipscomb, March 8, 1947, JRW.

20. P. W. Reynolds to J. R. Webb, 1945, JRW.

21. Holden, *Lambshead Before Interwoven,* 108.

22. P. W. Reynolds to J. R. Webb, 1945, JRW; J. R. Webb to Mary Southerland, March 8, 1947, JRW.

23. P. W. Reynolds to J. R. Webb, 1945, JRW.

24. Henry Griswold Comstock, "Some of My Experiences," HGC, 10.

25. U.S. Census, Stephens County, Tex., 1870.

CHAPTER 1

1. Comstock, "Some of My Experiences," HGC, 9–10; *The Galveston Daily News* of December 24, 1873, gave his name as "Elbert."

2. Comstock, "Some of My Experiences," HGC, 10.

3. Charles Goodnight, "The Killing of Oliver Loving," *The Trail Drivers of Texas,* ed. J. Marvin Hunter, 903–908; J. Evetts Haley, *Charles Goodnight,* 123, 170–73; Dan L. Thrapp, *Encyclopedia of Frontier Biography,* 3:1581. This story was incorporated into Larry McMurtry's successful novel and even more popular TV movie, *Lonesome Dove.* Brother Fayette found Bill Wilson, near death from hunger and thirst, along the trail (Sallie Reynolds Matthews, *Interwoven,* 55).

4. Haley, *Charles Goodnight,* 123.

5. Comstock, "Some of My Experiences," HGC, 13.

6. Ibid., 1.

7. Comstock was eighty-four years old in 1935 when he committed his memories of that drive to paper. The memoir remained in the family, read only by relatives, for some twenty years. Then family members presented a copy to Watt Matthews, patriarch of the Clear Fork cattle country and nephew of John Larn (Robert K. DeArment, "John Larn's Bloody Trail Drive," 17).

8. Comstock, "Some of My Experiences," HGC, 8.

9. Ibid., 8.

10. Ibid., 9.

11. Ibid., 11. Comstock consistently spelled his foreman's name "Laren."

12. Ibid., 12–13.

13. Ibid., 13.

14. Ibid., 16.

15. Ibid., 15.

16. Ibid., 16–17.

17. Ibid., 20.

18. Ibid., 21.

19. Pioneer Clear Fork cattleman Silas Hough, a partner of George T. Reynolds, had driven herds over the Pecos Trail for years (Vernon R. Maddux, *John Hittson*, 96–97).

20. Comstock, "Some of My Experiences," HGC, 27.

21. Ibid., 27.

22. Ibid., 29–30.

CHAPTER 2

1. Or "Arbour." Contemporary accounts spell the name both ways. Another source identifies the saloon owner as John Skelly ("Frontier Sketches," *Denver Field and Farm*, June 15, 1912).

2. *Colorado Chieftain*, February 15, 1872.

3. *Colorado Chieftain*, February 8, 1872.

4. Comstock, "Some of My Experiences," HGC, 31.

5. "Frontier Sketches," *Denver Field and Farm*, June 15, 1912.

6. Haley, *Charles Goodnight*, 205.

7. *Colorado Chieftain*, February 15, 1872.

8. *Colorado Chieftain*, February 8, 1872.

9. *Colorado Chieftain*, February 15, 1872.

10. Comstock, "Some of My Experiences," HGC, 31–32.

11. Ibid., 32.

12. Letter, John Hittson to William Veale, published in the *San Antonio Daily Express*, February 27, 1873, and quoted in Maddux, *John Hittson*, 73–74. Charles Goodnight put the figure at 300,000 (J. Evetts Haley, *The XIT Ranch of Texas*, 27).

13. First Lieutenant Sartle to commanding officer at Fort Stanton, March 5, 1872, Arrott collection; quoted in Maddux, *John Hittson*, 167.

14. Bill Reynolds, *Trouble in New Mexico,* 2:252.

15. Maddux, *John Hittson,* 161–62; Philip J. Rasch, "The Hittson Raid," 78.

16. Haley, *Charles Goodnight,* 206.

17. "Frontier Sketches," *Denver Field and Farm,* June 15, 1912. Five years later George Wilson was arrested and jailed at Pueblo, Colo., charged with the killing of Sheriff Tafoya. Newspapers described him as "one of the worst desperadoes in the country," and said he had murdered a sheriff in Texas and several other men. Lee Perkins, sheriff of Montague County, Tex., went to Pueblo in an attempt to have Wilson extradited for a murder in his county, but the Colorado authorities refused to turn him over, saying they would hang him there and also his brother Fayette if they could catch him. However, George escaped from the Pueblo hoosegow in June 1877 and was apparently never tried (*Dodge City Times,* June 9, 1877; Report of Lt. G. W. Campbell, Company B, Western Frontier Battalion, Texas Rangers, to Major John B. Jones, June 15, 1877, AGF).

18. "Frontier Sketches," *Denver Field and Farm,* June 15, 1912. According to this report both Fayette Wilson and Tom Atwell died in San Antonio at the hands of the notorious Texas gunfighter, John Wesley Hardin; but Hardin, who in his autobiography claimed responsibility for as many as forty killings, never mentioned either man in his list of victims, nor have any of Hardin's several biographers.

19. *Mesilla Valley Independent,* September 8, 1877; Frederick Nolan, *The Lincoln County War,* 153–54, 503.

20. Thrapp, *Encyclopedia of Frontier Biography,* 1:17.

21. Diron L. Ahlquist, letter to the author, August 12, 2001, quoting Guard Reports, November 17, 1871 to May 4, 1872; May 7, 1872 to November 4, 1872, FSM. According to the unverified story "Frontier Sketches" in *Denver Field and Farm,* June 15, 1912, Mason and Font Twombly, alias Parkinson, were both later killed in Kansas cowtowns—Mason in a rumpus at Newton, and Font at the hands of a man named Charles Codero in Wichita.

22. Sammy Tise, *Texas County Sheriffs,* 475.

23. Metz, *John Selman,* 40.

24. Ibid., 52–53.

25. Ibid., 22.

26. Ibid., 22.

27. Frank Collinson, *Life in the Saddle,* 93.

28. John P. Meadows to E. P. Lamborn, January 30, 1927, EPL.

29. Metz, *John Selman*, 34. John was the fourth and Tom the eighth child of Jeremiah and Permelia Selman (U.S. Census, Franklin County, Ark., 1850; Grayson County, Tex., 1860).

30. Tise, *Texas County Sheriffs*, 475.

31. Metz, *John Selman*, 45. John Selman, Jr. said that Larn and Selman combined their cattle and used the "Four of Clubs" brand. He hinted that the partners augmented their herd by means of cattle theft, saying they "adopted more modern methods [using] fast horses [and] long ropes" (John R. Selman, Jr., "John Selman of El Paso," interview by Franklin Reynolds, JRS, 46).

32. Blanton, *John Larn*, 12.

33. Metz, *The Shooters*, 232.

34. Blanton, *John Larn*, 12.

35. Holden, *Lambshead Before Interwoven*, 115.

36. The marriage license was issued on November 9, 1872, by W. Metcalf, clerk of the district court, Palo Pinto County; and the marriage conducted by C. K. Stribling, Minister of the Gospel (Palo Pinto County Court Records).

37. Blanton, *John Larn*, 13; Holden, *Lambshead Before Interwoven*, 111. The cottage was partially rebuilt and a new roof was added by the owners, the Putnam family. The gardens with their playing card designs were still plainly visible in 1999.

38. Blanton, *John Larn*, 13.

CHAPTER 3

1. This was probably one of the notorious Wilson brothers who had ridden with Larn in New Mexico. It may well have been Charlie, who narrowly escaped death at the hands of Larn seven months after returning to the Clear Fork area. Tom Atwell, another veteran of Larn's 1871 cattle drive, the Trinidad shooting, and the Hittson raid, also returned to the Clear Fork about this time and went to work for Larn.

2. Emmett Roberts, "Frontier Experiences," 44–46.

3. The names are taken from garbled and confused accounts in Comstock, "Some of My Experiences," HGC, 35; Drew Kirksey Taylor, *Taylor's Thrilling Tales*, 23–24; J. R. Webb, "Phin W. Reynolds," 20; John Chadbourne Irwin, "Frontier Life," JCI, 10; *Galveston Daily News*, December 24, 1873; *Fort Worth Weekly Democrat*, December 20, 1873.

4. Fort Griffin Post Reports for December 1873, NA; Ty Cashion, *A Texas Frontier*, 98–99; Holden, *Lambshead Before Interwoven*, 132; Charles M. Robinson III, *Frontier World*, 117; Metz, *John Selman*, 54.

5. Taylor, *Taylor's Thrilling Tales*, 23–24.

6. E. P. Turner to Post Adjutant, January 6, 1874, quoted in Cashion, *A Texas Frontier*, 99. In a 1947 letter, Shackelford County researcher J. R. Webb expressed his conviction that Larn "personally killed Bush and Snow, who knew his Colorado record," but added the admonition, "Don't quote me" (J. R. Webb to Mary Southerland, March 8, 1947, JRW).

7. *Galveston Daily News*, December 24, 1873.

8. Taylor, *Taylor's Thrilling Tales*, 24.

9. Comstock, "Some of My Experiences," HGC, 33.

10. Cashion, *A Texas Frontier*, 99; *Galveston Daily News*, December 24, 1873.

11. Richard Henry Pratt, *Battlefield and Classroom*, 59–60.

12. Taylor, *Taylor's Thrilling Tales*, 24.

13. Comstock, "Some of My Experiences," HGC, 33. In his sketch of Larn's life, Joseph Edwin Blanton, a Matthews family member and Larn apologist, never mentions the Bush Knob Massacre, dismissing Comstock's account as "hearsay and supposition," since Comstock was not personally present (Blanton, *John Larn*, 10). Comstock got the details of the tragedy from his brother James, who was a close friend of John Webb, one of the murdered men. Blanton also ignored reports of the murders from other sources, including Phin Reynolds, John C. Irwin, Drew Taylor, military records, and newspaper accounts.

14. *Fort Worth Weekly Democrat*, December 20, 1873.

15. Comstock, "Some of My Experiences," HGC, 34.

16. *Galveston Daily News*, December 24, 1873.

17. Taylor, *Taylor's Thrilling Tales*, 25.

CHAPTER 4

1. Quoted in John Marvin Hunter, *The Story of Lottie Deno*, 44.

2. *Galveston Daily News*, May 15, 1874, quoting the *Weatherford Times*.

3. *Galveston Daily News*, July 13, 1878.

4. Datelined Fort Griffin, February 27, 1874, the story appeared in the March 11 edition of the *Dallas Daily Herald* and the March 11 edition of the *Galveston Daily News*.

5. *Southern Intelligencer-Echo*, November 16, 1874.

6. Biggers, *Shackelford County Sketches*, 73, 80; Hunter, *The Story of Lottie Deno*, 30; Hervey E. Chesley, *Adventuring with the Old-Timers*, 49; J. R. Webb, "Henry Herron," 25. Henry C. Jacobs was a brother-in-law of Andrew Arnold Blevins, who rode west after some unpleasantness in Texas. Blevins probably spent time in Fort Griffin before taking part in a murky affair involving stolen horses, a reported killing, and an escape from the Texas Rangers. Under the name Andy Cooper he later turned up in Arizona, where he played a major role in the bloody Pleasant Valley War. On September 4, 1887, Commodore Perry Owens killed Blevins in a celebrated shootout at Holbrook, Ariz. (Webb, "Phin W. Reynolds," 137; Don Dedera, *A Little War of Our Own*).

7. Carl Coke Rister, *Fort Griffin*, 129; Irwin, "Frontier Life," JCI, 8.

8. Irwin, "Frontier Life," JCI, 8. It was Sallie Reynolds Matthews's recollection that Collins was hanged on the banks of the creek (*Interwoven*, 126). Don Biggers related a different tale, saying that Collins was murdered for his money, which supposedly was buried near the creek (*Shackelford County Sketches*, 41).

9. John C. Irwin remembered the lawyer's name as "King" ("Frontier Life," JCI, 7–8); Ben O. Grant recorded it as "Fisch" ("An Early History of Shackelford County," 86). Grant doubted that the vigilance organization had anything to do with the attorney's death; he suspected that the woman's husband and his friends committed the murder and pinned the OLM tag on the body to divert suspicion. The Old Law Mob is said to have originated in Palo Pinto County (Grant, "Citizen Law Enforcement Bodies," 158–59).

10. Grant, "Citizen Law Enforcement Bodies," 159.

11. Ibid., 159.

12. Rister, *Fort Griffin*, 129.

13. Irwin, "Frontier Life," JCI, 9.

14. Blanton, *John Larn*, 13.

15. Fort Griffin rivaled any camp in the West for toughness, but it is doubtful if even in its wildest days it ever reached the cesspool depths of debauchery and depravity depicted in Cormac McCarthy's mystical, poetic, and brutal 1985 novel, *Blood Meridian*.

CHAPTER 5

1. Roberts, "Frontier Experiences," 52.

2. Webb, "Henry Herron," 23.

3. Robinson, *Frontier World*, 73–74, 85.

4. Shackelford County District Court Docket, 1:4.

5. Shackelford County Commissioners' Court Minutes, 1:32 and 42, July 3, 1875.

6. One of those released was Joe Horner, a desperado who later changed his name and ways and, as Frank Canton, became a notable and highly respected peace officer in several states and territories (Robert K. DeArment, *Alias Frank Canton*, 321).

7. *Jacksboro Frontier Echo*, September 18, October 16, 1875.

8. *Galveston Daily News*, December 25, 1875. Edgar Rye, however, wrote that Brownlee stood trial for murder in Shackelford County and was later lynched with other members of an outlaw gang in 1876. (*The Quirt and the Spur*, 96, 101, 157).

9. William Steele, *A List of Fugitives from Justice*, (1878), 167. Ogelsby was also wanted in Grayson County on an 1877 swindling indictment (Ibid., 160).

10. Blanton, *John Larn*; Metz, *John Selman*, 55; Robinson, *Frontier World*, 120–21. A woman with an active imagination who lived in the house after Larn's death composed a manuscript in which she claimed to have discovered skeletons of his victims littering the surrounding yard and to have found secret places in the house where the ghost of Larn lurked with deadly weapons (Metz, *John Selman*, 212).

11. Sworn statement of J. M. Larn in application for certificate of occupancy, filed September 13, 1876, before J. N. Masterton, Shackelford county clerk. Appearing to testify to the truth of Larn's statement were J. H. Selman and M. V. Hoover, "credible and trustworthy citizens" (Shackelford County Property Records).

12. *Fort Worth Weekly Democrat*, June 19, 1875.

13. *San Antonio Daily Herald*, February 23, 1875.

CHAPTER 6

1. The origin of the appellation is not clear. It has been suggested that members when going into action put tin in their hatbands so they could be identified by other members (Robinson, *Frontier World*, 99–100).

2. J. E. Van Riper to John B. Jones, June 26, 1878. Van Riper's superior, Lt. G. W. Campbell, only ten days before had estimated the membership at about eighty (G. W. Campbell to John B. Jones, June 16, 1878). Lt. G. W. Arrington, who replaced Campbell at Fort Griffin, wrote Jones

on August 31, 1878, that he was "satisfied that at one time nearly everybody [in the Clear Fork country] belonged to the mob," AGF.

3. Biggers, *Shackelford County Sketches*, 42.

4. Collinson, *Life in the Saddle*, 93.

5. Robinson, *Frontier World*, 139.

6. J. E. Van Riper to John B. Jones, June 15, 1878, AGF.

7. Rye, *The Quirt and the Spur*, 114–15.

8. Grant, "An Early History of Shackelford County." Other county officers elected: W. H. Ledbetter, judge; J. N. "Jack" Masterton, clerk of the county and district courts; R. A. Jeffress, attorney; John A. "Bud" Matthews, assessor; J. H. Stegall, treasurer; G. A. Kirkland, surveyor; and M. F. Barber, cattle and hide inspector (*Galveston Daily News*, March 16, 1876). There were only 320 votes cast in this election, but because there were only 455 residents of the county enumerated in the 1875 state census, virtually every male voted.

It was not unusual for a man so young to serve as county sheriff in those frontier times. Voters recognized that men still in their twenties brought a boldness and fearlessness to the position that was essential. In Jones County, just west of Shackelford County, George A. Scarborough was only a month past his twenty-fifth birthday when he was elected sheriff in 1884. Ira Aten was only twenty-six when he served as sheriff of Fort Bend County, Tex., during the violent "Jaybird" and "Woodpecker" feud of 1889. Up in Kansas, W. B. "Bat" Masterson was twenty days short of his twenty-fourth birthday when he was elected sheriff of vast Ford County in 1877.

9. *Jacksboro Frontier Echo*, March 3, 1876; Shackelford County Commissioners' Court Minutes, 1:66–67; Tise, *Texas County Sheriffs*, 462. Elected officials entrusted with county funds were required to post bond.

10. Ty Cashion identifies "Comanche Jim" as James W. Grahame, an "English drifter," (*A Texas Frontier*, 194, 330).

11. Conflicting reports of the date appeared in the papers. In his story published in the *Fort Worth Weekly Democrat* of April 22, 1876, Lone Star gave the date as Wednesday, April 5. The *Dallas Daily Herald* story of April 29, 1876, gave it as Sunday, April 9.

12. *Fort Worth Weekly Democrat*, April 22, 1876.

13. Rister, *Fort Griffin on the Texas Frontier*, 155–56, quoting the *Dallas Daily Herald*, April 29, 1876.

14. Rister, *Fort Griffin*, 156, quoting an 1880 book, *Ten Years in Texas*.

15. Wayne Gard, *Frontier Justice*, 203, quoting the *Dallas Daily Herald*, April 23, 1876. P. W. Reynolds named Bill Howsley as one of the vigilantes

who lynched the man, "locally known as a thief [who] went by the name of Doc McBride. [He] was shot and wounded by the crowd and then the next morning was found hanging" (Webb, "Frontier History Notes," JRW).

16. As partners in the cattle business between 1871 and 1882, John Oatman Dewees and James F. Ellison drove more than 400,000 head of cattle from Texas to the northern markets. In 1875 and 1876 Bill Bishop was also a partner in the firm (Jimmy M. Skaggs, *The Cattle-Trailing Industry*, 61).

17. Fort Griffin Post Report for April 1876. Capt. Theodore Schwan, 11th Infantry, to Adjutant General, April 11, 1876, NA; *Galveston Daily News*, April 26, 1876.

18. *Fort Worth Weekly Democrat*, April 22, 1876. Phin Reynolds remembered the site as being in Stonewall, the next county west of Haskell (P. W. Reynolds to J. R. Webb, March 8, 1947, JRW).

19. Henry W. Strong, *My Frontier Days*, 78.

20. *Jacksboro Frontier Echo*, April 14, 1876; Rister, *Fort Griffin*, 156, quoting the *Dallas Daily Herald*, April 29, 1876. A dispatch from Denison printed in the *Galveston Daily News* of April 14, 1876, reported that "four men have been hanged at Fort Griffin, and *two* are in jail for horse stealing. Shooting and such like amusements make it quite live[ly] in that frontier town [italics mine]." Phin Reynolds simply said the posse "disposed of the three men in the shinnery" (P. W. Renolds to J. R. Webb, March 8, 1947, JRW).

21. *Fort Worth Weekly Democrat*, April 22, 1876.

22. Both Henry Strong (*My Frontier Days*, 78) and Phin Reynolds (P. W. Reynolds to J. R. Webb, Match 8, 1947, JRW) named Lt. E. P. Turner as the officer who accompanied Larn on this expedition. However, it is clear from Captain Schwan's April 11 letter to the Adjutant General that Shipman led the detail (NA). The Fort Griffin Post Reports for April also indicate that Lt. Turner was on detached duty at Fort Concho during this period (NA). Strong and Reynolds both apparently confused this affair with the Bush Knob Massacre three years earlier in which Turner did participate with Larn.

23. Shackelford County Commissioners' Court Minutes, 1:99; *Fort Worth Weekly Democrat*, April 29, 1876.

24. *Jacksboro Frontier Echo*, April 28, 1876. The man's name was given as "Fraughts" in this paper and "Foughts" in the *Dallas Daily Herald* of April 29, 1876. The *Echo* of June 16, 1876, reported that a case brought by the state against "Houston Faught" pending in the district court had been "dismissed by plaintiff, Faught having been hung by a vigilance

committee." Author Charles Robinson has questioned why the military authorities would allow Faught to be taken by a mob from the fort's hospital (*Fort Griffin*, 107); but the man was not a military prisoner, and it is evident from the military involvement in the Bush Knob and Watson killings that the Army approved of, and was complicit in, extreme action by determined civilians against outlaws.

25. *Jacksboro Frontier Echo*, April 28, 1876.

26. Ibid., April 28, 1876.

27. Ibid., June 2, 1876.

28. Ibid., June 2, 1876. No record of extradition papers for Henderson or Floyd can be found in the Texas State Archives (Donaly E. Brice to the author, September 20, 1999). The Dodge City papers made no mention of Henderson, Floyd, or Larn's visit. The *Galveston Daily News* reported erroneously on June 8, 1876, that one of Larn's prisoners was Kansas Bill, who was evidently one of the few Henderson gang members to escape the wrath of the Clear Fork vigilantes.

29. *Jacksboro Frontier Echo*, May 12, 1876.

30. *Fort Worth Weekly Democrat*, April 29, 1876. "Long Kate" was probably Kate Gamble, or "Indian Kate," whose shanty on the Clear Fork was a notorious outlaw hangout. Kate and Ellen Gentry, if they ever left The Flat, soon returned. Both later paid fines for fighting and vagrancy (Rister, *Fort Griffin*, 139; Robinson, *Fort Griffin*, 73–74; *Fort Griffin Frontier Echo*, September 20, 1879). Sally Watson was of course the "widow" of Joe Watson. "Pony" Spencer may have been Lark Ferguson, a Texas desperado who as "Pete Spence" or "Peter Spencer" later became infamous in Arizona. Tom Riley departed Griffin for Jacksboro, where he was soon arrested and jailed, charged with the stabbing murder of Patrick McPeak on March 26, 1876. He escaped on July 22, 1876. Evidently Jack County Sheriff Lee Crutchfield did not want him back very badly; he offered only a $15 reward for his capture (*Jacksboro Frontier Echo*, July 28, 1876).

31. *Dallas Daily Herald*, April 29, 1876.

32. *Jacksboro Frontier Echo*, June 30, 1876.

33. Ibid., June 9, 1876. Shackelford County historian J. R. Webb termed the numbers "a wild exaggeration" (J. R. Webb to Mary Southerland, March 8, 1947, JRW).

34. *Galveston Daily News*, June 18, 1876.

35. Ibid., June 8, 1876.

36. *Galveston Daily News*, June 4, 1876.

37. *Jacksboro Frontier Echo*, June 9, 1876. Henry Herron, who had just arrived in Shackelford County from his native Wisconsin, recalled seeing the

prisoners in the new courthouse. "They looked pretty tough to me," he said. "The next morning they were hanging on an elm tree. . . . It impressed me that it was a good idea to leave the other fellow's horses alone" (Henry Herron to J. R. Webb, July 17, 1940, JRW).

38. *Galveston Daily News,* June 4, 8, 1876; *Houston Daily Telegraph,* June 15, 1876.

39. *Austin Weekly Statesman,* June 22, 1876.

40. Rye, *The Quirt and the Spur,* 101. Rye seems to have been mistaken about Brownlee. See chapter 5.

41. Seth Hathaway, "The Adventures of a Buffalo Hunter," 135.

42. *Jacksboro Frontier Echo,* May 12, 1876.

43. Ibid., March 8, 1878.

44. Ben O. Grant, "Life in Old Fort Griffin," 35–36.

45. Webb, "Frontier History Notes," JRW; P. W. Reynolds to J. R. Webb, 1945, JRW.

46. *Galveston Daily News,* June 18, 1876.

47. Rye, *The Quirt and the Spur,* 102.

48. Ibid., 106.

49. *Jacksboro Frontier Echo,* May 19, 1876.

50. Ibid., June 9, 1876.

51. *Fort Worth Weekly Democrat,* April 29, 1876.

52. *Galveston Daily News,* June 7, 1876.

53. Webb, "Frontier History Notes," JRW; P. W. Reynolds to J. R. Webb, 1945, JRW.

54. Grant, "An Early History of Shackelford County."

55. Irwin, "Frontier Life," 12.

56. *Fort Worth Weekly Democrat,* April 22, 1876.

57. Ibid., April 29, 1876.

58. Ibid., April 29, 1876.

59. *Galveston Daily News,* July 15, 1876.

60. Grant, "Life in Old Fort Griffin," 34–35.

61. Irwin, "Frontier Life," 13.

62. *Galveston Daily News,* June 3, 1876.

63. Contract of sale, February 2, 1876, Shackelford County Deed Records.

64. Blanton, *John Larn,* 13–14.

65. Larn purchased Lots One and Two in Block Number Three (Deed of Conveyance, February 29, 1876, notarized by C. K. Stribling and witnessed by W. R. Cruger, Shackelford County Deed Records). Selman had purchased the lots in November 1875, for $150 (Metz, *John Selman,* 64).

66. Hoover, having married Mattie Matthews, Mary Jane Larn's sister, was another Larn brother-in-law (Matthews, *Interwoven*, 106).

67. Throckmorton County Deed Records.

68. Contract of sale, August 24, 1876, Throckmorton County Deed Records. John and Tom Selman witnessed the sale.

69. *Galveston Daily News*, September 29, 1876.

70. Recorded November 22, 1876, Shackelford County Deed Records.

71. *Fort Worth Daily Democrat*, September 2, 1876. No doubt the bootlegger called "Jack" Greathouse in this story was "Whiskey Jim" Greathouse, notorious in The Flat for his liquor trade with the Indians. An associate of "Larapie Dan" Moran and Dan McClusky, who were lynched by the Tin Hats earlier in the year, Whiskey Jim Greathouse would figure prominently in the criminal career of "Billy the Kid" Bonney in New Mexico a few years later (Philip J. Rasch, *Warriors of Lincoln County*, 88–97).

72. *Jacksboro Frontier Echo*, August 18, 1876.

73. In all likelihood the man whose life Larn twice saved that day was old buffalo hunter Joe McCombs himself. When he spoke of Larn's death fifty-eight years later, McCombs broke down and cried. "He was one of the best friends I ever had," he said. "He saved my life once and if I could, I would have done as much for him" (Grant, "An Early History of Shackelford County"). The rescue may appear to have been out of character for Larn, but he was probably motivated less by compassion for a drunk than by a shared hatred for the black Yankee soldiers at the fort. Like the drunk, he was an unreconstructed Rebel. He had clearly demonstrated on the cattle drive to Colorado that he was a violent racist. He used the bluecoats at the fort when they served his purposes, as in the Bush Knob massacre, but he undoubtedly held them in contempt.

74. *Fort Worth Daily Democrat*, December 19, 1876. Lone Star's story was repeated in the *Galveston Daily News* of December 26 and the *Austin Weekly Statesman* of December 28.

75. Cashion, *A Texas Frontier*, 218–19.

76. Collinson, *Life in the Saddle*, 67–68.

77. John R. Cook, *The Border and the Buffalo*, 225–26.

CHAPTER 7

1. A. P. "Ott" Black, *The End of the Long Horn Trail*, 13.

2. Biggers, *Shackelford County Sketches*, 29.

3. Jim McIntire, *Early Days in Texas,* 65

4. Black, *The End of the Long Horn Trail,* 15.

5. J. Marvin Hunter, ed., *The Trail Drivers of Texas,* 203; Wayne Gard, *The Chisholm Trail,* 217–18.

6. Newt Jones to J. R. Webb, March 15, 1947, JRW.

7. Ibid.

8. John Meadows to J. Evetts Haley, June 13, 1935, JEH.

9. Webb, "Phin W. Reynolds," 126–27.

10. Donnelly was married to Lucinda Selman, Old John's sister (Karen Holliday Tanner, *Doc Holliday,* 97).

11. Collinson, *Life in the Saddle,* 85.

12. Hunter, *The Story of Lottie Deno,* 41.

13. "Special Telegram" in the *Galveston Daily News,* January 20, 1877. In other accounts the name is given as "Barron." The story of the shooting was also covered in the *Jacksboro Frontier Echo,* January 19, 1877; the *San Antonio Daily Express,* January 24, 1877; and the *Galveston Daily News,* January 27, 1877. Lt. G. W. Campbell of the Texas Rangers gave the bare details in a report to Maj. John B. Jones, January 31, 1877, AGF.

14. W. Hubert Curry, *Sun Rising on the West,* 132.

15. Still conscious, Jeffress felt his life's blood draining from his body. When the American Indian woman who did his laundry came by, he had her bring his clean shirts and stuff them around the wounds to slow the bleeding. Those who came in the morning to bury him were amazed to find him still alive. Friends took him by hack and train to his Virginia home where he recuperated (P. C. Jeffress to J. R. Webb, September 14, 1960, JRW). Jeffress later returned to Shackelford County. Newt Jones remembered seeing him in a wheelchair a year after the gunfight (Newt Jones to J. R. Webb, March 15, 1947, JRW).

16. Newt Jones to J. R. Webb, March 15, 1947, JRW. At least one newspaper account alleged that Reed, as "proved by his position" in the saloon, "must have killed the young man Barrow" (*Galveston Daily News,* January 27, 1877).

17. *Dallas Daily Herald,* January 25, 1877.

18. Newt Jones to J. R. Webb, March 15, 1947, JRW.

19. Rye, *The Quirt and the Spur,* 104–105. Drew Kirksey Taylor mentions the shooting and also names Selman's victim as "Collins" (*Taylor's Thrilling Tales,* 25), but he was writing after the publication of Rye's book and may have drawn on it for details.

20. Biggers did not identify either Larn or Selman by name, but made it clear who they were when he said "the sheriff was a long time chief in

the vigilance committee, at whose hands he afterward met his death, and the deputy was later killed by one of his kind in El Paso" (Biggers, *Shackelford County Sketches*, 42).

21. Collinson, *Life in the Saddle*, 94.

22. J. P. Meadows to E. P. Lamborn, January 30, 1927, EPL.

23. Shackelford County Court Minutes, 1:112. "It was generally believed in the community that [Larn] was in sympathy with Bland in the [Bee Hive] fight, resented the killing, and resigned in protest over the killing by his deputy, W. Cruger" (Newt Jones to J. R. Webb, March 15, 1947, JRW). Larn resigned on March 7, 1877, coincidentally the date that the story of the Hampton killing appeared in the *Galveston Daily News*.

24. Cruger had helped establish the new town south of Griffin that became the seat of Shackelford County. At his suggestion, it was named Albany after his hometown (Biggers, *Shackelford County Sketches*, 74).

25. Mrs. A. A. Clarke to C. L. Sonnichsen, June 6, 1944, CLS.

26. Newt Jones to J. R. Webb, March 15, 1947, JRW.

27. "As part of the oath of office, both men solemnly swore that they had never fought a duel with deadly weapons or acted as a second" (Metz, *John Selman*, 72–73, citing the Shackelford County Records of Official Bonds, B:54–63).

28. Metz, *John Selman*, 73.

29. First Sergeant Kissinger to John B. Jones, May 15, 1877; Company B Monthly Return for May 1877, AGF.

30. John Meadows to J. Evetts Haley, June 13, 1935, JEH.

31. Cora Melton Cross, "Recollections of Bob Lauderdale," 325.

32. Contracts of sale, Throckmorton County Deed Records.

33. Deed of conveyance, N. F. Barber to John M. Larn, May 25, 1877; Deed of conveyance, John M. Larn to B. Marks, May 28, 1877, both deeds notarized by C. K. Stribling, Shackelford County Deed Records.

34. Quoted in Walter Prescott Webb, "Buffalo Hunt," 36.

35. *Jacksboro Frontier Echo*, September 10, November 11, 1875.

36. Rye, *The Quirt and the Spur*, 76.

37. Report of Scouts, Monthly Returns for June 1877, Company B, Frontier Battalion, Texas Rangers, AGF.

38. Ibid., July 1877.

39. Ibid., August 1877.

40. *Jacksboro Frontier Echo*, August 24, 1877.

41. *Austin Weekly Statesman*, September 27, 1877.

42. G. W. Campbell to John B. Jones, September 30, 1877, AGF.

43. Steele, *A List of Fugitives from Justice*, 167.

44. Chesley, *Adventuring with the Old-Timers,* 93.

45. G. W. Campbell to John B. Jones, June 16, 1878, AGF.

46. Frank Collinson, "Three Texas Trigger Man," FCP.

47. Collinson, *Life in the Saddle,* 55.

48. Chesley, *Adventuring with the Old-Timers,* 93.

49. Rye, *The Quirt and the Spur,* 76–77.

50. *Fort Worth Daily Democrat,* April 17, 1877; G. W. Campbell to John B. Jones, April 30, 1877, AGF; Metz, *John Selman,* 74.

51. Metz, *John Selman,* 64–65. In the Shackelford County Deed Record Book, the property, for which Selman reportedly paid $200, was described as "one box house, 12 x 14 ft [and] one bureau, one bedstead, four chairs, one wash stand" (Shackelford County Deed Records).

52. Metz, *John Selman,* 79.

53. John Meadows to J. Evetts Haley, June 27, 1933, JEH.

54. Ibid., June 13, 1935.

55. Ibid.

56. Ibid.

57. Ibid., June 27, 1933.

58. Ibid.

59. Ibid., June 13, 1935.

60. Ibid. It is interesting that Hunt Kelly, who may have saved the lives of Larn and Selman at this time, was the same man who had, with Selman, put up bonds for Hurricane Bill Martin a year earlier.

CHAPTER 8

1. Quoted in Robinson, *Frontier World,* 123.

2. John Meadows to J. Evetts Haley, June 13, 1935, JEH.

3. *Galveston Daily News,* July 13, 1878.

4. John Meadows to J. Evetts Haley, June 27, 1933, JEH. Meadows consistently identified the stone masons as brothers, but was less certain as to their names. In 1933 he recalled the surname as "Lewis" at one point and "Stewart" at another. When he was interviewed again two years later (June 13, 1935), he said their name was "Williams." Another Fort Griffin veteran, Frank Lloyd, in a 1939 interview remembered the two victims as "Irishmen" Larn and Selman were taking to town when "they killed them and throwed them in Blue Hole there" (Frank Lloyd to J. Evetts Haley, June 12, 1939, JEH.

5. Collinson, "Three Texas Trigger Men," FCP.

6. J. E. Van Riper to John B. Jones, June 15, 1878, AGF. In his book Edgar Rye gave the names "Wilks" and "Jones" to the missing stone masons (*The Quirt and the Spur*, 112).

7. *Galveston Daily News*, July 13, 1878.

8. John Meadows to J. Evetts Haley, June 27, 1933 JEH. Some thought the deceased was a man named "Cupp," but Texas Ranger Alex Hutchison later saw Cupp, very much alive, in Oklahoma (Newt Jones to J. R. Webb, March 15, 1947, JRW).

9. P. W. Reynolds to J. R. Webb, 1945, JRW.

10. Robinson, *Frontier World*, 125.

11. Irwin, "Frontier Life," JCI, 10.

12. Newt Jones to J. R. Webb, March 15, 1947, JRW.

13. G. W. Campbell to John B. Jones, February 26, 1878, AGF. Edgar Rye, in recounting this incident, greatly exaggerated the number of hides found, saying there were two hundred (Rye, *The Quirt and the Spur*, 107). Sophie A. Poe repeated this fiction in her biography of her husband, John Poe (*Buckboard Days*, 90).

14. Newt Jones to J. R. Webb, March 15, 1947, JRW.

15. *Galveston Daily News*, July 13, 1878.

16. *San Antonio Daily Herald*, March 19, 1878.

17. Report of Scouts, Monthly Returns for March 1878, Company B, Frontier Battalion, Texas Rangers, AGF; J. E. Van Riper to John B. Jones, April 3, 1878, AGF.

18. G. W. Campbell to John B. Jones, April 3, 1878, AGF.

19. *Fort Worth Daily Democrat*, February 20, 1878.

20. G. W. Campbell to John B. Jones, April 3, 1878, AGF.

21. Ibid.

22. Letter and petition from citizens of Throckmorton County to John B. Jones, May 26, 1878, AGF.

23. J. R. Fleming to R. B. Hubbard, May 1, 1878, AGF.

24. John B. Jones to G. W. Campbell, May 7, 1878, AGF.

25. Special Order No. 131, May 18, 1878, AGF.

26. Letter and petition from citizens of Throckmorton County to Maj. John B. Jones, May 26, 1878, AGF.

27. Telegram, W. F. Baird, M.D., and S. K. Smith, D.D.S., to John B. Jones, May 31, 1878, AGF.

28. *Galveston Daily News*, July 13, 1878.

29. Cashion, *A Texas Frontier*, 230.

30. J. E. Van Riper to John B. Jones, June 15, 1878, AGF.

31. John R. Selman, "John Selman of El Paso," JRS.

32. Bill of Sale, Throckmorton County Deed Records, May 15, 1878. The sale was notarized by Justice of the Peace J. S. Steele and witnessed by Tom Cat Selman and Tom Curtis.

33. G. W. Campbell to John B. Jones, June 16, 1878, AGF.

34. Lawrence Clayton, letter to the author, March 3, 1992. John Chadbourne Irwin was the grandfather of Mr. Clayton's wife.

35. Metz, *John Selman*, 85. Metz was told this story in 1964 by Dave Richards, Treadwell's grandson (Ibid., 216).

36. Fifteen Day Report, J. E. Van Riper to John B. Jones, June 15, 1878, AGF.

37. J. E. Van Riper to John B. Jones, June 15, 1878, AGF.

38. G. W. Campbell to John B. Jones, June 16, 1878, AGF.

39. Rye, *The Quirt and the Spur*, 107.

40. Cause No. 26, Shackelford County Justice of the Peace Court.

41. Members of Cruger's posse were named by Phin Reynolds and Newt Jones in interviews with J. R. Webb in the 1940s. George Reynolds was married to Mary Larn's sister, Lucinda; Ben Reynolds was married to one of her cousins (Blanton, *John Larn*). Bill Gilson, who by all accounts was a close friend and confidant of John Larn, probably went along reluctantly.

42. Accounts of the events of June 21–24 almost always include this Paul Revere ride by Minnie Martin and indicate it was a solitary effort. Sam Baldwin recalled that Blue Roberts, the ex-Ranger, accompanied the woman (Chesley, *Adventuring with the Old-Timers*, 93).

43. Rye, *The Quirt and the Spur*, 108. John Poe's wife, in *Buckboard Days* (92–93), repeats this account as she purportedly heard it from her husband, but it has obviously been taken, almost word for word, from Rye's book.

44. Phin Reynolds to J. R. Webb, March 8, 1947, JRW.

45. Newt Jones to J. R. Webb, March 15, 1947, JRW.

46. *Galveston Daily News*, July 13, 1878.

47. Newt Jones to J. R. Webb, March 15, 1947, JRW; Holden, *Lambshead Before Interwoven*, 152; Robinson, *Frontier World*, 133.

48. Collinson, *Life in the Saddle*, 96.

49. Metz, *John Selman*, 87–88; Robinson, *Frontier World*, 133.

50. Phin Reynolds to J. R. Webb, July 28, 1944, JRW.

51. Cause No. 26, Shackelford County Justice of the Peace Court.

52. Report of Scouts, Monthly Returns for June 1878, Company B, Frontier Battalion, Texas Rangers, AGF.

53. *Fort Worth Daily Democrat*, June 26, 1878; *Galveston Daily News*, June 26, 1878; *Jacksboro Frontier Echo*, July 5, 1878.

54. Newt Jones to J. R. Webb, March 15, 1947, JRW.

55. Ibid.

56. Rye, *The Quirt and the Spur*, 109–10.

57. Webb, "Henry Herron," 29.

58. *Albany News*, June 6, 1930; Mollie Moore Godbold, "Comanche and the Hardin Gang," 263–65.

59. Slack gave the time as "between twelve and one," Cruger, "about one o'clock," and Poe, "about two o'clock" ("Report of Inquisition into Death of John M. Larn, June 24, 1878").

60. Ibid.

61. *Albany News*, June 6, 1930; Godbold, "Comanche and the Hardin Gang," 265.

62. "Report of Inquisition into Death of John M. Larn, June 24, 1878."

63. Robinson, *Frontier World*, 138.

64. *Albany News*, June 6, 1930; Godbold, "Comanche and the Hardin Gang," 265.

65. Collinson, *Life in the Saddle*, 95–96.

66. "Report of Inquisition into Death of John M. Larn, June 24, 1878." It is said that when the body was examined, a partially healed gunshot wound in the arm was discovered. Evidently this had been inflicted by a Granger during one of Larn's recent raids (*Galveston Daily News*, July 13, 1878).

67. Phin Reynolds to J. R. Webb, 1945, JRW.

68. John Meadows, interview by J. Evetts Haley, June 13, 1935, JEH. John Alexander "Bud" Matthews was Mary Larn's brother. Martin Van Buren "Mart" Hoover had married Martha Ann Matthews, Mary's sister.

69. Collinson, "Three Texas Trigger Men," FCP.

70. *Fort Worth Daily Democrat*, July 2, 1878. The story was told by Special Deputy Sheriff W. O. Beach of Palo Pinto County, who was in Albany at the time of Larn's killing or immediately thereafter. Beach went on to Breckenridge where on June 25 he related the tale to Sigma, who passed it on to the *Democrat*.

71. Telegram, Jim McIntire to John B. Jones, June 24, 1878, AGF.

72. Report of Scouts, Monthly Returns for June 1878, Company B, Frontier Battalion, Texas Rangers, AGF.

73. *Jacksboro Frontier Echo*, July 5, 1878.

74. McIntire, *Early Days in Texas*, 63.

75. Ibid., 63–64.

76. Report of Scouts, Monthly Returns for June 1878, Company B, Frontier Battalion, Texas Rangers, AGF.

77. Newt Jones to J. R. Webb, March 15, 1947, JRW.

78. John Meadows to J. Evetts Haley, June 27, 1933, JEH.

79. Ibid., June 13, 1935.

80. Telegram, W. R. Cruger to John B. Jones, June 30, 1878, AGF.

81. John B. Jones to G. W. Arrington, July 13, 1878, AGF. Listed were Drs. W. T. Baird and S. K. Smith, Frank Conrad, J. S. Wright, C. K. Stribling, A. J. Lancaster, "Old Man" (Joseph B.) Matthews, "the Treadwells" (H. R. and James H.), J. M. Cupp, William Brisky, George A. Kirkland, J. M. Doughtery, Judge (W. H.) Ledbetter, George Mathis (Mathews), "Old Man" (Jules) Hervey, and "Old Man" (T. E.) Jackson.

82. Telegrams and letters, G. W. Arrington to John B. Jones, July 31, August 1, August 15, 1878, AGF.

83. G. W. Arrington to John B. Jones, August 31, 1878, AGF.

AFTERWORD

1. In 1999 someone climbed the fence around the grave and glued down four coins—a quarter, a dime, a nickel, and a penny, a total of forty-one cents—on the base of the stone. The significance of the act is a mystery, but it has been suggested that the coins refer to the .41 caliber pistol Larn may have carried (Julia Putnam, interviewed by the author, January 4, 2000).

2. Charles A. Siringo, *Riata and Spurs*, 171.

3. J. R. Webb to Mary Southerland, March 8, 1947, JRW.

4. The stock was sold for $8,480 (Throckmorton County Cause No. 94, *J. B. Matthews vs. John Brown*, Throckmorton County District Court Dockets). The 1880 tax records show that the Larn property consisted of two 160-acre surveys, fifteen head of horses and mules valued at $190, and two hundred head of cattle, valued at $1,625.

5. Deposition of J. B. Matthews in a suit he later brought against Brown (Throckmorton County Cause No. 94).

6. Matthews, *Interwoven*, 168–69; Blanton, *John Larn*, 27.

7. Only one of the Brown children, a daughter named Mary, was alive in 1947 when J. R. Webb contacted her in California. She and her two grown children, like many residents of the Clear Fork country, resented anything "derogative to the character" of Mary Jane's first husband (J. R. Webb to Mary Southerland, March 8, 1947, JRW).

8. Throckmorton County Cause No. 36, In the Matter of the Guardianship of Willie A. Brown, Minor. In assuming the guardianship responsibility, Matthews furnished bond in amount of $20,000. Bill Howsley and Phin Reynolds were witnesses.

9. Throckmorton County Cause No. 94, *J. B. Matthews vs. John Brown*, Throckmorton County District Court Dockets. The plaintiff affirmed that John Larn, when he died intestate, "left a large community estate, inherited and owned by said widow, Mary Larn and William Larn, now called William Brown, share and share alike," and that William was entitled to $4,240 (half of the cattle sale proceeds), plus interest compounded at 8 percent per annum, a total of $7,790.

10. Throckmorton County Deed Records, 9:214.

11. Rev. John Brown, *Twenty-Five Years a Parson in the Wild West*, 166–75.

12. Ibid., 166.

13. Ibid., 210.

14. J. R. Webb to Mary Southerland, March 8, 1947, JRW.

15. Robinson, *Frontier World*, 145.

16. Sonnichsen, *I'll Die Before I'll Run*, 166.

17. Blanton, *John Larn*, 21–22. The article in the June 6, 1930, issue of the *Albany News*, was by "W. S. Adair," who quoted R. A. Slack—one of the guards at the time of the Larn lynching—throughout. Slack identified John Selman by name but did not once mention the name of John Larn. It is clear, however, to whom he was referring.

18. Sonnichsen, *I'll Die Before I'll Run*, 166.

19. Robinson, *Frontier World*, 145; James A. Browning, *Violence Was No Stranger*, 136.

20. Throckmorton County Deed Records, 9:255; *Ex Parte W. A. Brown*, District Court, Throckmorton County, May 17, 1899.

21. J. R. Webb to Mary Southerland, March 8, 1947, JRW.

22. Harry Wheeler to Sims Ely, October 24, 1907, quoted in Bill O'Neal, *The Arizona Rangers*, 122.

23. Harry Wheeler to Gov. Joseph H. Kibbey, January 11, 1908, quoted in O'Neal, *The Arizona Rangers*, 201–202.

24. Blanton, *John Larn*, 37.

25. J. R. Webb to Mary Southerland, March 8, 1947, JRW.

26. Browning, *Violence Was No Stranger*, 136.

27. Robinson, *Frontier World*, 145.

28. Julia Putnam, letter to the author, February 2, 2000. The current family members plan on celebrating one hundred years of ownership in the year 2006.

29. *Fort Griffin Frontier Echo,* June 4, 1881.

30. Ibid., January 21, 1882.

31. Ron Tyler, *The New Handbook of Texas,* 4:146–49.

32. Ibid., 5:555–58; Matthews, *Interwoven,* 156, 185.

33. Poe, *Buckboard Days;* Tyler, *The New Handbook of Texas,* 5:248–49.

34. R. K. DeArment, "John Shanssey: From Prize Ring to Politics."

35. *San Antonio Daily Express,* September 15, 17, 1878; February 15, March 1, 1879; Harold Hutton, *Doc Middleton,* 65–67; Wayne C. Lee, *Wild Towns of Nebraska,* 85–87.

36. Sam Baldwin interview in Chesley, *Adventuring with the Old-Timers,* 94.

37. Collinson, "Three Texas Trigger Men," FCP.

38. Waldo Koop to the author, April 19, 1982.

39. *Dodge City Times,* July 12, 1881.

40. Horace Jones, *The Story of Early Rice County,* 135–36.

41. *Fort Griffin Frontier Echo,* August 2, 1879; Grant, "Life in Old Fort Griffin," 33.

42. Tise, *Texas County Sheriffs,* 490.

43. *Fort Worth Daily Democrat,* February 9, 1882.

44. Jess G. Hayes, *Apache Vengeance,* 89–96.

45. Rollie Burns, "Reminiscences of 56 Years," RBM; Webb, "Henry Herron," 31.

46. *Fort Griffin Frontier Echo,* July 3, 1880.

47. Ibid., July 31, 1880.

48. *Albany (Tex.) Star,* January 12, 1883; *Albany (Ga.) Courier-Journal,* January 19, 1883.

49. *Fort Griffin Frontier Echo,* April 26, June 14, 1879, October 1, 1881; Webb, "Henry Herron," 31; James M. Draper file, JDF.

50. *Fort Griffin Frontier Echo,* October 1, December 10, 1881; Barbara A. Neal Ledbetter, *Fort Belknap,* 207–12, 223, 229.

51. Charlie Siringo, who claimed to know Merrill well, said he was at the head of the organization (*Riata and Spurs,* 171).

52. Phin Reynolds to J. R. Webb, 1945, JRW; Matthews, *Interwoven,* 130–31; Metz, *John Selman,* 127; Siringo, *Riata and Spurs,* 171.

53. Skelton Glenn manuscript, quoted in Metz, *John Selman,* 128.

54. R. N. Mullin, "Selman's Early Life," 3; Metz, *John Selman,* 94–95.

55. Siringo, *Riata and Spurs,* 171–73.

56. Metz, *John Selman,* 94.

57. John Selman, Jr., "John Selman of El Paso," JRS.

58. Siringo, *Riata and Spurs,* 171.

59. John Meadows to E. P. Lamborn, January 30, 1927, EPL.

60. Metz, *John Selman*, 108.

61. John Meadows to J. Evetts Haley, June 13, 1935, JEH.

62. R. K. DeArment, "The Great Outlaw Confederacy," 14–19.

63. Metz, *John Selman*, 93.

64. Telegram, L. B. Caruthers to John B. Jones, June 22, 1880, TSA; J. Evetts Haley, *Jeff Milton*, 62–63; Sonnichsen, *I'll Die Before I'll Run*, 164–65.

65. W. R. Cruger to John B. Jones, July 2, 1880, AGF.

66. *Fort Griffin Frontier Echo*, September 11, 1880.

67. Phin Reynolds to J. R. Webb, 1945, JRW.

68. Metz, *John Selman*, 93–94.

69. Ibid., 93–94; Robert K. DeArment, *George Scarborough*, 144–50, 154–56.

70. John Meadows to J. Evetts Haley, June 27, 1933, JEH.

71. J. R. Webb to Mary Southerland, March 8, 1947, JRW.

72. John Meadows to J. Evetts Haley, June 13, 1935, JEH.

73. Holden, *Lambshead Before Interwoven*, 157.

Bibliography

GOVERNMENT DOCUMENTS

Arrott Collection, District of New Mexico, Letters, Record Group 98, Vol. 45, 405, National Archives, Washington, D.C.

Fort Griffin, Tex., Post Reports and Correspondence, Record Group 393, National Archives, Washington, D.C. (NA).

Fort Sill, Okla., Guard Reports, Nov. 17, 1871–May 4, 1872; May 7, 1872–Nov. 4, 1872, Fort Sill Museum Archives (FSM).

Palo Pinto County, Tex., Court Records.

"Report of Inquisition into Death of John M. Larn, June 24, 1878," Shackelford County, Tex.

Shackelford County, Tex., Commissioners' Court Minutes.

Shackelford County, Tex., Deed Records.

Shackelford County, Tex., District Court Dockets.

Shackelford County, Tex., Records of Official Bonds.

Throckmorton County, Tex., Deed Records.

Throckmorton County, Tex., District Court Dockets.

U.S. Census Reports. 1850: Franklin County, Ark.; 1860: Calhoun County, Ala.; Grayson County, Tex.; 1870: Shackelford County, Tex., Stephens County, Tex.; 1880: Shackelford County, Tex.

BOOKS

Beshoar, Barron B. *Hippocrates in a Red Vest: The Biography of a Frontier Doctor*. Palo Alto, Calif.: American West Publishing Company, 1973.

Beshoar, M., M.D. *All About Trinidad and Las Animas County, Colorado*. Denver: Times Steam Printing House and Blank Book Manufactory, 1882.

Biggers, Don H. *Shackelford County Sketches*. 1908. Reprint edited and annotated by Joan Farmer, Albany and Fort Griffin, Tex.: Clear Fork Press, 1974.

Black, A. P. "Ott." *The End of the Long Horn Trail*. Selfridge, N.Dak.: Selfridge Journal, [1936?].

Blanton, Joseph Edwin, and Watt Reynolds Matthews. *John Larn*. Albany, Tex.: Venture Press, 1994.

Brown, Rev. John. *Twenty-Five Years a Parson in the Wild West: Being the Experience of Parson Ralph Riley*. Fall River, Mass.: n.p., 1896.

Browning, James A. *Violence Was No Stranger: A Guide to the Grave Sites of Famous Westerners*. Stillwater, Okla.: Barbed Wire Press, 1993.

Cashion, Ty. *A Texas Frontier: The Clear Fork Country and Fort Griffin, 1849–1887*. Norman: University of Oklahoma Press, 1996.

Chesley, Hervey E. *Adventuring with the Old-Timers—Tales Told*. Midland, Tex.: Nita Stewart Haley Memorial Library, 1979.

Collinson, Frank. *Life in the Saddle*. Norman: University of Oklahoma Press, 1963.

Cook, John R. *The Border and the Buffalo*. Topeka, Kans.: Crane & Co., 1907.

Curry, W. Hubert. *Sun Rising on the West: The Saga of Henry Clay and Elizabeth Smith*. Crosbyton, Tex.: Quality Printers and Typographers, 1979.

DeArment, Robert K. *Alias Frank Canton*. Norman: University of Oklahoma Press, 1996.

_____. *George Scarborough: The Life and Death of a Lawman on the Closing Frontier*. Norman: University of Oklahoma Press, 1992.

Dedera, Don. *A Little War of Our Own: The Pleasant Valley Feud Revisited*. Flagstaff, Ariz.: Northland Press, 1988.

Fugate, Francis L., and Roberta B. Fugate *Roadside History of New Mexico*. Missoula, Mont.: Mountain Press Publishing Company, 1989.

Gard, Wayne. *Frontier Justice*. Norman: University of Oklahoma Press, 1949.

_____. *The Chisholm Trail*. Norman: University of Oklahoma Press, 1957.

Haley, J. Evetts. *Charles Goodnight: Cowman and Plainsman*. Norman: University of Oklahoma Press, 1949.

_____. *Jeff Milton: A Good Man With a Gun.* Norman: University of Oklahoma Press, 1948.

_____. *The XIT Ranch of Texas and the Early Days of the Llano Estacado.* Norman: University of Oklahoma Press, 1953.

Hardin, John Wesley. *The Life of John Wesley Hardin.* 1896. Reprint, Norman: University of Oklahoma Press, 1961.

Hayes, Jess G. *Apache Vengeance.* Albuquerque: University of New Mexico Press, 1954.

Holden, Frances Mayhugh. *Lambshead Before Interwoven: A Texas Range Chronicle 1848–1878.* College Station: Texas A&M University Press, 1982.

Holden, W. C. *Rollie Burns: Or An Account of the Ranching Industry on the South Plains.* 1932. Reprint, College Station: Texas A&M University Press, 1986.

Hunter, John Marvin. *The Story of Lottie Deno.* Bandera, Tex.: Four Hunters, 1959.

_____, ed. The Trail Drivers of Texas. . . . Project directed by Geore W. Saunders. 1924. Reprint, Austin: University of Texas Press, 1985.

Hutton, Harold. *Doc Middleton: Life and Legends of the Notorious Plains Outlaw.* Chicago: The Swallow Press, 1974.

Jones, Horace. *The Story of Early Rice County.* Lyons, Kans.: Lyons Daily News Plant, 1959.

Ledbetter, Barbara A. Neal. *Fort Belknap Frontier Saga: Indians, Negroes, and Anglo-Americans on the Texas Frontier.* Burnet, Tex.: Eakin Press, 1982.

Lee, Wayne C. *Wild Towns of Nebraska.* Caldwell, Idaho: The Caxton Printers, Ltd., 1988.

McCarthy, Cormac. *Blood Meridian: Or the Evening Redness in the West.* New York: Random House, 1985.

McIntire, Jim. *Early Days in Texas: A Trip to Hell and Heaven.* 1902. Reprint edited and annotated by Robert K. DeArment, Norman: University of Oklahoma Press, 1992.

Maddux, Vernon R. *John Hittson: Cattle King on the Texas and Colorado Frontier.* Niwot, Colo.: University Press of Colorado, 1994.

Matthews, Sallie Reynolds. *Interwoven: A Pioneer Chronicle.* 1936. Reprint, Austin and London: University of Texas Press, 1977.

Metz, Leon. *John Selman: Texas Gunfighter.* 1966. Reprint, Norman: University of Oklahoma Press, 1980.

_____. *The Shooters.* El Paso, Tex.: Mangan Books, 1976.

Miller, Joseph, ed. *The Arizona Rangers.* New York: Hastings House, Publishers, Inc., 1972.

Miller, Rick. *Sam Bass & Gang.* Austin: State House Press, 1999.

Nolan, Frederick. *The Lincoln County War: A Documentary History.* Norman and London: University of Oklahoma Press, 1992.

O'Neal, Bill. *The Arizona Rangers.* Austin: Eakin Press, 1987.

————. *Encyclopedia of Western Gunfighters.* Norman: University of Oklahoma Press, 1979.

Poe, Sophie A. *Buckboard Days.* Caldwell, Idaho: The Caxton Printers, Ltd., 1936.

Pratt, Richard Henry. *Battlefield and Classroom: Four Decades with the American Indian, 1867–1904.* Lincoln and London: University of Nebraska Press, 1964.

Rasch, Philip J. *Warriors of Lincoln County.* Stillwater, Okla.: The National Association For Outlaw and Lawman History, Inc., 1998.

Reynolds, Bill. *Trouble in New Mexico: The Outlaws, Gunmen, Desperadoes, Murderers And Lawmen for Fifty Turbulent Years, Volumes 1–3.* Bakersfield, Calif.: Privately published, 1994–95.

Rister, Carl Coke. *Fort Griffin on the Texas Frontier.* Norman: University of Oklahoma Press, 1956.

Robinson, Charles M., III. *The Buffalo Hunters.* Austin: State House Press, 1995.

————. *The Frontier World of Fort Griffin.* Spokane, Wash.: The Arthur H. Clark Company, 1992.

Rye, Edgar. *The Quirt and the Spur.* 1909. Reprint, Austin: Steck-Vaughn Company, 1967.

Siringo, Charles A. *Riata and Spurs.* Boston and New York: Houghton Mifflin Company, 1927.

Skaggs, Jimmy M. *The Cattle-Trailing Industry.* Norman and London: University of Oklahoma Press, 1991.

Sonnichsen, C. L. *I'll Die Before I'll Run: The Story of the Great Feuds of Texas.* New York: Devin-Adair Company, 1962.

Steele, William. *A List of Fugitives from Justice.* Austin: Adjutant General's Office, State of Texas, 1878.

Strong, Henry W. *My Frontier Days and Indian Fights on the Plains of Texas.* N.p., [1926?].

Tanner, Karen Holliday. *Doc Holliday: A Family Portrait.* Norman: University of Oklahoma Press, 1998.

Taylor, Drew Kirksey. *Taylor's Thrilling Tales of Texas.* N.p., 1926.

Thrapp, Dan L. *Encyclopedia of Frontier Biography,* 4 vols. Glendale, Calif.: Arthur H. Clark, 1988–94.

Tise, Sammy. *Texas County Sheriffs.* Albuquerque: Oakwood Printing, 1989.

Tyler, Ron, ed. *The New Handbook of Texas,* 6 vols. Austin: The Texas State Historical Association, 1996.

Wilson, Laura. *Watt Matthews of Lambshead.* Austin: The Texas State Historical Association, 1989.

ARTICLES

Cross, Cora Melton. "Recollections of Bob Lauderdale: A Life on the Open Cattle Range of Texas." *Frontier Times* (May, 1929): 325.

DeArment, Robert K. "The Great Outlaw Confederacy." *True West* 37 (September 1990): 14–19.

———. "'Hurricane Bill' Martin, Horse Thief." *True West* 38 (June 1991): 38–45.

———. "John Larn's Bloody Trail Drive." *True West* 44 (January 1997): 17–22.

———. "John Shanssey: From Prize Ring to Politics." *True West* 46 (March 1999): 25–29.

———. "Kreeger's Toughest Arrest." *True West* 33 (June 1986): 14–19.

———. "Toughest Cow Outfit in Texas (Part One)." *True West* 38 (April 1991): 26–30.

Godbold, Mollie Moore. "Comanche and the Hardin Gang." *Southwestern Historical Quarterly* LXVII: 55–77, 247–66.

Grant, Ben O. "Citizen Law Enforcement Bodies: A Little More About the Vigilantes." *West Texas Historical Association Year Book* 39 (1963): 155–61.

———. "Life in Old Fort Griffin." *West Texas Historical Association Year Book* 10 (1934): 32–41.

Hathaway, Seth. "The Adventures of a Buffalo Hunter." *Frontier Times* (December 1931: 105–12, 129–35.

Holden, W. C. "Law and Lawlessness on the Texas Frontier, 1875–1890." *Southwestern Historical Quarterly* XLIV: 188–203.

Mullin, R. N. "Robert Mullin, Noted Authority of Period, Gives His Version of Selman's Early Life." *The Southwesterner* (June 1964): 3–6.

Rasch, Philip J. "The Hittson Raid." *Brand Book of the New York Posse of the Westerners* 10 (1963): 77–78, 86

Roberts, Emmett. "Frontier Experiences of Emmett Roberts of Nugent, Texas." *West Texas Historical Association Year Book* 3 (June 1927): 43–58.

Robinson, Charles M. III. "Buffalo Hunting at Fort Griffin." *True West* 35 (March 1988): 20–27.

_____. "John Larn." *True West* 36 (October 1989): 21–27.

Selman, John Henry. "Harden Had 'Four Six-Guns' to Beat." *The South-westerner* (June 1964): 2, 12, 17–19.

Selman, John R., Jr. "John Selman." Interview by Franklin Reynolds. *All Western Magazine*, (November 1935): 45–61.

Webb, J. R. "Chapters from the Frontier Life of Phin W. Reynolds." *West Texas Historical Association Year Book* 21 (1945): 110–43.

_____. "Henry Herron, Pioneer and Peace Officer During Fort Griffin Days." *West Texas Historical Association Year Book* 20 (1944): 21–50.

Webb, Walter Prescott. "Buffalo Hunt." *True West* 8 (January–February 1961): 36.

NEWSPAPERS

Albany (Ga.) Courier-Journal, January 19, 1883.

Albany (Tex.) News, June 6, 1930.

Albany (Tex.) Star, January 12, 1883.

Austin Weekly Statesman, June 22, December 28, 1876; September 27, 1877.

Colorado Chieftain (Pueblo), February 8, 15, 1872.

Dallas Daily Herald, March 8, 1874; April 23, 29, 1876; January 25, 1877.

Dallas Morning News, January 12, 1992.

Denver Field and Farm, June 15, 1912.

Dodge City Times, June 9, 1877; July 12, 1881.

Fort Griffin Frontier Echo, April 20, 26, June 14, 1879; August 2, September 20, 1879; March 3, July 3, 31, September 11, October 30, 1880; June 4, October 1, December 10, 1881; January 21, 1882.

Fort Worth Daily Democrat, September 2, December 19, 1876; April 17, 29, June 22, July 26, 1877; February 20, 21, June 26, July 2, 1878; February 9, 1882.

Fort Worth Weekly Democrat, December 20, 1873; June 19, 1875; April 22, 29, 1876.

Galveston Daily News, December 24, 1873; March 11, May 15, 1874; December 25, 1875; March 16, April 2, 14, 26, June 2, 3, 4, 7, 8, 14, 18, 26, July 15, 29, September 29, December 26, 1876; January 20, 27, March 7, 1877; June 26, July 13, 1878.

Houston Daily Telegraph, June 15, 1876.

Jacksboro Frontier Echo, September 10, 18, October 16, November 11, 1875; March 3, April 14, 28, May 12, 19, June 2, 9, 16, 30, July 28, August 18, 1876; January 19, August 24, 1877; March 8, July 5, 1878.

Mesilla Valley Independent, September 8, 1877.
San Antonio Daily Express, February 27, 1873; January 24, 1877; September
     15, 17, 1878; February 15, March 1, 1879.
San Antonio Daily Herald, February 23, 1875; March 19, 1878.
Southern Intelligencer-Echo (Austin), November 16, 1874.

UNPUBLISHED MATERIALS

Adjutant General's Files. Archives Division, Texas State Library and
     Archives, Austin (AGF).
Ahlquist, Diron L. Letter to author, August 12, 2001.
Brice, Donaly E. Letter to author, September 20, 1999.
Burns, Rollie. "Reminiscences of 56 Years." Manuscript in Nita Stewart
     Haley Memorial Library, Midland, Tex. (RBM).
Clayton, Lawrence. Letter to author, March 3, 1992.
Collinson, Frank. "Three Texas Trigger Men." Manuscript in Frank
     Collinson Papers, Historical Research Center, Panhandle-Plains His-
     torical Museum, Canyon, Tex. (FCP).
Comstock, Henry Griswold. "Some of My Experiences and Observations
     on the Southwestern Plains of 1871 and 1872." Old Jail Art Center
     and Archive, Albany, Tex. (HGC).
James M. Draper File. Old Jail Art Center and Archive, Albany, Tex.
     (JDF).
Eckhart, C. F. Letter to author, January 14, 1999.
Grant, Ben O. "An Early History of Shackelford County." Master's thesis,
     Hardin-Simmons University, Abilene, Tex.
J. Evetts Haley Collection. Nita Stewart Haley Memorial Library, Mid-
     land, Tex. (JEH)
Irwin, John Chadbourne. "Frontier Life of John Chadbourne Irwin." Edit-
     ed by Hazel Best Overton. Manuscript in Historical Research Center,
     Panhandle-Plains Historical Museum, Canyon, Tex. (JCI).
Koop, Waldo. Letter to author, April 19, 1982.
E. P. Lamborn Collection. Kansas State Historical Society, Topeka (EPL).
Metz, Leon. Letter to author, July 28, 1996.
Robert E. Nail, Jr. Collection. Old Jail Art Center and Archive, Albany,
     Tex.
Putnam, Julia. Letters to author, August 18, September 28, 1996; Febru-
     ary 2, 14, 2000.
_____. Interview by author, January 4, 2000.

Robinson, Charles III. Letter to author, June 17, 1992.

Selman, John R., Jr. "John Selman of El Paso." Manuscript in Texas State
    Library, Austin (JRS).

Dr. C. L. Sonnichsen Papers. University of Texas at El Paso (CLS).

Texas Ranger Frontier Battalion Records. Texas State Archives, Austin
    (TSA).

J. R. Webb papers. Rupert Richardson Research Center, Hardin-Simmons
    University Library, Abilene, Tex. (JRW).

Index